AF584231

The Joy of Connections

Dr Ruth K Westheimer broke stigmas for more than forty years, beginning in the 1980s with her nationally syndicated US radio show *Sexually Speaking*. She authoured or co-authoured forty-six books on many topics, and was named New York's Ambassador to Loneliness, the first such position in the United States. A beloved therapist known to millions as 'Dr Ruth', she died in July 2024.

the joy of connections

100 ways to beat
loneliness and live
a happier and more
meaningful life

Dr Ruth K. Westheimer

with Allison Gilbert *and* Pierre Lehu

Melbourne | London | Minneapolis

Scribe Publications
18–20 Edward St, Brunswick, Victoria 3056, Australia
2 John St, Clerkenwell, London, WC1N 2ES, United Kingdom
3754 Pleasant Ave, Suite 100, Minneapolis, Minnesota 55409, USA

Published by Scribe 2024
This edition published by arrangement with Rodale Books, an imprint of Random House, a division of Penguin Random House LLC

Internal pages designed by Susan Turner

Printed and bound in the UK by CPI Group (UK) Ltd, Croydon CR0 4YY

Scribe is committed to the sustainable use of natural resources and the use of paper products made responsibly from those resources.

Scribe acknowledges Australia's First Nations peoples as the traditional owners and custodians of this country, and we pay our respects to their elders, past and present.

978 1 761381 31 7 (Australian edition)
978 1 915590 53 4 (UK edition)
978 1 761385 90 2 (ebook)

Catalogue records for this book are available from the National Library of Australia and the British Library.

scribepublications.com.au
scribepublications.co.uk
scribepublications.com

To Miriam, Joel, and their families—RW

To Mark, Jake, and Lexi—AG

To Joanne—PL

It is not good for a human being to be alone.

—Genesis 2:18

Contents

Introduction

LONELINESS IS ABOUT THE QUALITY OF CONNECTIONS in your life, not the quantity.

Unlike solitude, which can be sought-after and peaceful, loneliness stems from a sense of social isolation. You might be surrounded by people from morning to night, but if you feel invisible to them, like you don't matter, you will likely feel alone. Similarly, if you believe that you have nobody to call in an emergency or to water your plants when you go on vacation, you might feel particularly adrift and disconnected.

The reason loneliness is painful is that human beings are social creatures by nature and our health depends on these relationships. When we're lonely, serious health conditions may arise. Loneliness is associated with an increased risk of stroke, confusion and memory loss, and cardiovascular disease. It may shorten our lives, as much as smoking up to fifteen cigarettes a day, and is even more harmful than being sedentary and significantly overweight.

But loneliness is subjective. It's a *feeling*. And because it's a feeling, there's plenty we can do to alleviate it.

You can make the decision that being lonely is no longer an option. You can pursue relationships that make you feel special and appreciated. I want you to know that it's possible to choose a fuller, richer path right now.

I know this is true from my work and my life. And it's why at age ninety-six I couldn't sit idly by when so many are suffering. If you've sunk into the swamp of loneliness, you may feel like it's impossible to get out. Take my hand. Let me pull you out of the muck.

When New York State governor Kathy Hochul appointed me Ambassador to Loneliness, the first such position in the United States, she couldn't have chosen someone with better credentials. I've been sleeping with loneliness my entire life.

I've known the loneliness of being separated from my family at the age of ten, becoming a refugee, and never seeing my parents or grandparents again. I've known the loneliness of illness and disability, the kind that crashes over you when your body has been pierced by shrapnel and you've been severely wounded in a bomb blast, have lost part of your foot, and are sure you're about to die. I've also known the loneliness of feeling unchangeably other. While my four-foot-seven height has always been a punch line on late-night television, and while being shorter than most everyone else has surely helped me stand out professionally, it's also been profoundly isolating. I often thought that no man would ever want me and that I'd never get married. But I did manage to get married, three times, in fact. The first two marriages ended in divorce and the third, to Fred Westheimer, lasted thirty-five years, until he passed away; he was the love of my life.

I'll let you in on a little secret: My personal experiences with loneliness aren't the only reasons I was named Ambassador to Loneliness. The appointment happened because I lobbied for it. I pushed for the role because I knew that my background as a sex therapist made me uniquely qualified to help people overcome loneliness. Sexual dysfunction and loneliness both carry stigma. Nobody is excited to admit they're having difficulty in the bedroom. Nobody is thrilled to confess they have too few reliable friends. Shame is the thread that connects them both, and shame is what I've always tried to help people overcome. Think back to the 1980s. The humiliation gay people felt during the AIDS crisis was wholly avoidable. It's why I always spoke so openly about homosexuality, embracing all expressions of love. I tried hard to change the conversation about sex and belonging during *that* epidemic, and I know that if we talk openly about loneliness—unapologetically and without euphemisms—those who are feeling painfully disconnected will feel less alone, too.

That loneliness is now an epidemic is widely known. Studies have been done and books have been written. Media coverage has exposed the vastness of the problem. I applaud all those who've undertaken this reporting and research. But, as I've mentioned, I offer a different and much-needed perspective. This is not a book about how society has arrived at such a tender and precarious place. This is not a book that examines the government's efforts to resolve the crisis (though at the end of this book U.S. Surgeon General Dr. Vivek Murthy offers important strategies for feeling more socially connected).

My training is as a behavioral therapist. When I saw clients in my office, I didn't spend time delving into their past, trying to figure out the root cause of their sexual problems. I left that to the psychologists and psychiatrists. My work was much more direct and fast-moving. I simply helped anyone who came to see me—or listened to me on the radio or watched me on TV—have better sex by modifying how they engaged in sex. And this is the approach that I am taking with *The Joy of Connections*. If you are lonely, what you need is practical advice on beating back this scourge, and this is what I am going to provide.

The Joy of Connections offers a straightforward road

map for overcoming loneliness—one hundred concrete ideas and opportunities that can be acted upon immediately. The guidance is based on tactics I've used myself and in my private practice, some with clients who were quite lonely. I also include lessons from organizational psychologist and Wharton professor Adam Grant; founding director of the MIT Initiative on Technology and Self, Sherry Turkle; bestselling author and *Happier* podcast host Gretchen Rubin; and others.

But I'm not only giving you advice. I'm going to do the best I can to push you into *taking my advice*.

I'm going to be a cheerleader, a coach, and a drill sergeant, all rolled into one. Everyone who knows me quickly finds out that when I want something, I want it now, maybe even yesterday. Of course, some things you have to wait for, but in my life, I've found that waiting patiently often means that you don't get what you want. And since having some chutzpah is what it takes to make it in this world, we must apply this same type of agency to the problem of loneliness. Because while loneliness is a terrible thing, as I can attest to, it's also a condition that can be beaten back. And while I would never say that it will be easy, I will absolutely state that it's possible.

Dr. Ruth's Menu for Connection

SIMILAR TO THE COLORFUL PLATE THE USDA USES TO recommend which food groups should be consumed for a healthy lifestyle, my Menu for Connection represents the parts of our life that require the most care and attention for building and nurturing meaningful relationships. I created this simple framework to translate decades of scholarly research on human connections and happiness into guidance that you can use right now.

Instead of fruits, grains, vegetables, protein, and a small serving of dairy, I've developed one hundred empowering ideas and strategies and divided eighty-eight of them into five parts: "Self," "Family," "Friends and Lovers," "Community," and a small portion of "Technology." Each is an essential element of the Menu for Connection. The final twelve strategies are presented in "Your Monthly Calendar"

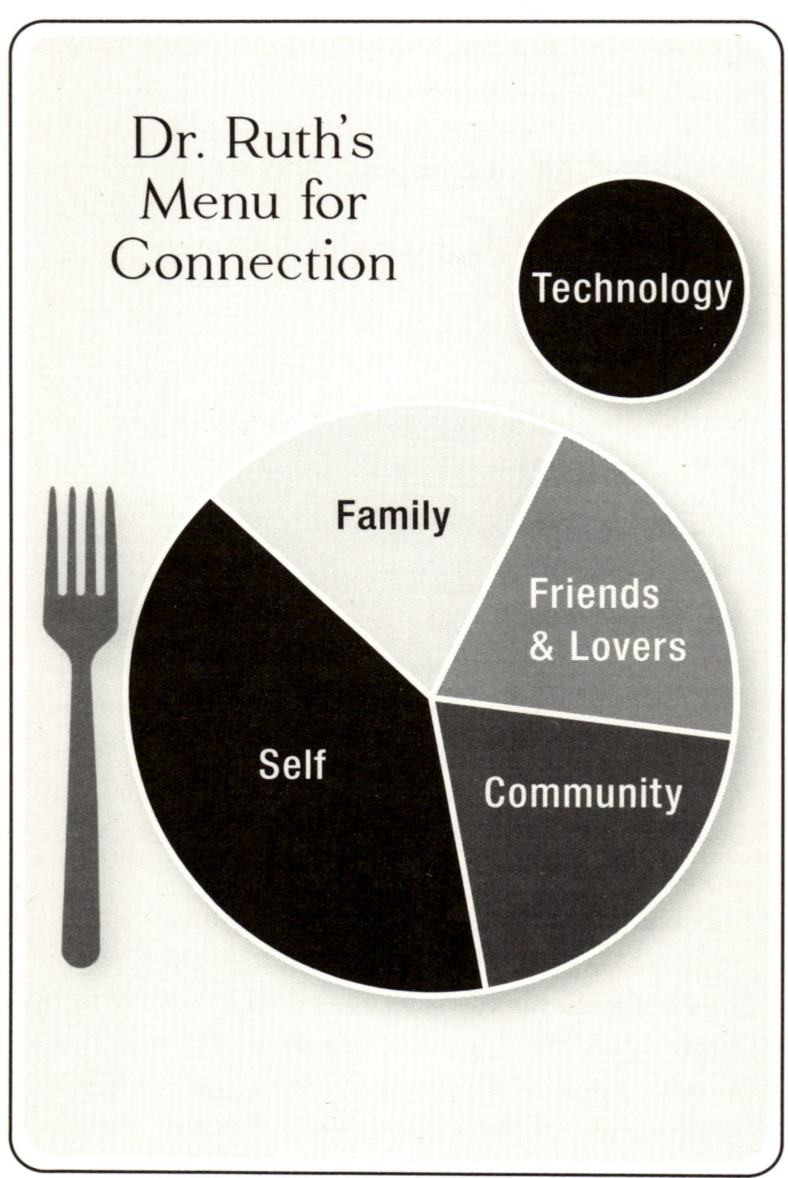
Dr. Ruth's
Menu for
Connection
Technology
Family
Friends
& Lovers
Self
Community

because there are times of the year that offer specific opportunities for building joy and relationships.

While I will explain each portion of the Menu for Connection at the opening of each section, it is important to note that the largest piece, the one that purposefully contains the most opportunities, is "Self." If you are struggling with loneliness and are ready to make positive changes in how you interact with others, you must first determine what it is about your outlook or behavior that has made you retreat into yourself or push people away. This is not easy to do, but your relationships are more likely to flourish once you put in the work.

Loneliness is an individual experience, and I recognize that each and every page may not resonate, as what's obvious to you might be illuminating and life-changing to someone else. Some concepts are for those who need help finding and making connections; others are for individuals who already have connections but want help deepening them. My hope is that you'll take away what you need and transform your relationships based on the cumulative nature of the Menu for Connection.

Let's get to work!

Self

WHILE IT MAY SEEM THAT EVERYONE AROUND you is fulfilled by their relationships, the truth is that most people experience loneliness at some point in their lives. Let that sink in. It's likely that most everyone you know, everyone in your neighborhood, everyone you walk by on the street, has felt the pangs of loneliness. A recent Meta-Gallup survey shows that nearly one in four adults around the world—more than one billion people—don't feel fully connected to others.

Ever since U.S. Surgeon General Dr. Vivek Murthy proclaimed loneliness an epidemic in the United States, there's been a flurry of activity to help people feel less alone. Legislation has been introduced in Congress to establish an Office of Social Connection Policy to advise the president. The World Health Organization launched the Commission on Social Connection. Mayors across the country have demanded funding to support more mental health programs in their cities and the staff to run them. And New York State governor Kathy Hochul appointed me Ambassador to Loneliness!

I lost my family in the Holocaust, and I could not have felt any lonelier because of that. While eventually I created a family in the typical sense, finding a life partner and having children and grandchildren, I never stopped pulling together a wider "chosen" family. I curated these bonds with absolute purpose. I went out of my way to find these friends and knit them together. And in doing so I became less lonely.

But getting to that point was hard. I grew up in an orphanage and was surrounded every minute of every day by other children. There was no privacy whatsoever! Yet on July 12, 1945, I confessed in my diary:

Above all, I'm longing for a friend.

And the next day, I wrote:

I live with 150 people—and am alone.

I now know what my seventeen-year-old self didn't yet understand. Loneliness has nothing to do with the number of people around you. If you're not meaningfully connected, if there's no substance to your interactions, you will likely feel insignificant and unseen. But you can bring loneliness to its knees. Unlike a fatal disease, loneliness, I've learned, is curable.

In my view, the key to ridding your life of loneliness resides inside you. As a therapist, I've sat across from many clients who faced very real hardships and disabilities, and I was able to help most of them. But I could never make the kinds of changes they needed *for* them; I could only *guide* them. Therapists are expert advisers. It's the individual seeking a new road who must take action.

But changing patterns of behavior takes effort. And this is why "Self" is the most important component of the Menu for Connection. You must pay attention to your thoughts, feelings, and actions, the ones that are holding you back from making the types of connections you most want. Self-awareness leads to coping strategies and solutions, builds self-esteem and confidence, and smooths communication with others so that you can nurture and maintain healthy relationships. With reflection, you're able to identify areas for improvement and follow through with your aspirations.

So let's begin by focusing our attention where it's likely the hardest and most uncomfortable, but also where success is solely within your power: on yourself.

Look in the Mirror

The first step to fixing any problem is to admit that it exists. If loneliness is what is affecting you, then what better way to face your problem than to stand in front of a mirror and say it out loud? You may feel silly, you may cry, but having the problem out in the open is your first step toward making the necessary changes to become less lonely. Reading this book is proof to me that you're aware of what's causing you pain and you're open to solutions. I have no doubt you're on your way to building the kinds of connections you most want!

I've faced many difficult challenges in my life, as you'll come to see as you read on. During a visit to Paris, where I had studied psychology at the Sorbonne in the early 1950s, I saw in a shop a ruby-red decorative sign for sale that immediately caught my eye. The words "It CAN be done" were emblazoned in English across the front in bright gold lettering. I didn't buy it, but the owner of the store later sent it to me as a gift. He had noticed how much I admired it. The sign has been my treasure ever since, for more than forty years. I look at it whenever I feel discouraged.

What's the difference between complaining to yourself that you're lonely and saying it out loud? I've been a therapist throughout my career and can tell you that my clients began to heal the moment they admitted to having a problem. The road ahead will be hard, but just keep going. You are getting closer to feeling less alone and isolated. *It CAN be done.*

Make Peace with Yourself

You will not be able to sustain healthy relationships if you don't love yourself first. No friend or sexual partner can do all that emotional heavy lifting for you, and worse, you might build walls around yourself that are so high that you'll prevent anyone from scaling them.

I am not suggesting you brainwash yourself into thinking that you're a gorgeous model if you're not, and I am not asking you to ignore physical or mental disabilities that make your life more difficult. Brushing off hardship is not what I'm saying to do. My advice is to gradually accept what makes you different and begin relationship-building from there. To do this—and I realize that I am biased as a lifelong therapist—you might consider professional counseling.

As I write these words, I do, in fact, love myself, but I had a very hard time being OK with who I was when I was young. When I was seventeen years old, in 1945, I started the diary I mentioned earlier. I was exceptionally lonely back then, in part because I felt utterly unattractive. *I'm so short, dumb, and ugly,* I brooded. *If I were normally grown, everything, everything would be much simpler.* Being four foot seven put me so far outside the realm of normal that I was shocked to learn many years later that I was able to become pregnant. I thought carrying a child would be biologically impossible. (After having two children, and now four grandchildren, I'm still overjoyed that my fear was misplaced!)

If you struggle with a disability, loving yourself will be easier if you recognize the obstacles society puts in the way of your efforts to deepen friendships and have sex. If you're a young woman and your friends are getting dressed together before heading to a party, you likely can't join them in the same taxi or Uber if you're confined to a wheelchair. (Or maybe you won't even go because you worry you won't be able to maneuver around the crowd.) Similarly, if you live in a group home, it's likely there are no locks on your door and it's impossible to have the kind of privacy that's conducive to intimacy.

You must accept your reality. Focus instead on what makes you exceptional. Mental and physical differences don't diminish your value. Only after I began to appreciate how smart I was and how advanced I was in school did I recognize that regardless of my height, I was worthy of love. I want the same for you.

Evaluate Your Routine

Self-assessment is critical. If you're not honest with yourself, it's unimaginable that you'll ever make the kinds of life-improving changes you want, no matter if you're longing for more friends or more sex. The more miserable you feel, the greater the need to acknowledge that your own choices are likely contributing to your loneliness.

Let's say you have a stressful job and so every night you turn on your television to find some mind-numbing relaxation. And while you're watching, you forget how lonely you are, and that's a relief. But you're not making friends sitting on your couch. Being passively entertained is a Band-Aid. It's OK, but it will never make loneliness go away.

I know how easy it is to fall into this kind of unhelpful, peopleless trap. After my husband of thirty-five years, Fred Westheimer, passed away, I thought about moving out of the apartment we'd shared for so many decades. I believed that a change of scenery would make me miss him less. But after looking at new places to live, I realized that my feelings of loneliness wouldn't go away just because I was looking at a different set of walls. I'd be missing Fred all the same, just in a different apartment. Slowly I began to understand that a new address would just be another kind of Band-Aid. What I really needed to do was pay greater attention to how I was spending my time. *Instead of apartment hunting, I should be people hunting. I should be inviting friends over or going out for the evening*. People would make me feel better and less alone—not real estate. And they did.

So how do you convince yourself that one or two nights a week you're going to participate in some activity that could lead to making friends or deepening connections instead of watching Netflix? By coming to terms with the seriousness of your situation in relation to loneliness. By paying attention to the times you usually opt to be alone and gradually replacing them with opportunities for social connection. This reckoning must be your motivation for getting out of the house.

Analyze Your Appearance

Note that in the first pages of this section I told you to take a hard look at yourself in the mirror. While the goal there was to make a psychological assessment of how you're doing in the connections-making and connections-keeping departments, while you're at it, give yourself a physical once-over, too.

If you look very lonely—if your hair's a mess, if you always have a frown on your face—it's going to be harder to make new friends. Should you be judged only on your appearance? Of course not, but it's part of human nature to do it anyway, so your first step toward making friends includes looking more approachable.

When I was a young woman, I didn't have a lot of money to buy many new blouses and pants. Plus, for two years I lived on two kibbutzim in Israel, and part of communal living means being more concerned about the welfare of the group than of yourself, including your clothes. But when I started to get noticed in the 1980s, right as my radio program *Sexually Speaking* exploded and I began making television appearances, Pierre Lehu, one of the co-authors of this book and my media director for more than forty years (I call him my minister of communications!), thought it was time for me to pay attention to how strangers were seeing me. I needed to look as kind and pleasant as possible so my advice on using contraception would be easier for people to hear. Pierre would ask me before every live and taped show if I'd gotten my hair done and what I was wearing. I became much more aware of how I presented myself. Every time I got dressed up, I'd call the transformation my "Pierre-ish look."

Consider buying some new clothes. You don't have to spend a lot—going to a thrift or vintage store is a great idea. Select shirts and sweaters that match how you want to feel. Push yourself to choose bright colors. If we deliberately act cheery when we're feeling down, there's a chance we'll actually become happier. The same can be said for the influence clothes and jewelry can have on our mood.

Be Selfish

People are often criticized for taking care of themselves. Or those who do take care of themselves often feel terribly guilty about it. Either way, there are times when you absolutely must put yourself first. (This is true even when you're living on a kibbutz.) And it's perfectly OK to be selfish.

Here's an example.

You have an elderly parent who requires a lot of attention. You've been providing this attention, and because of your ongoing presence, your social life has evaporated and you're feeling lonely. If you're an only child, you may feel stuck and need to come up with a creative solution to give yourself a break. But assuming you have siblings, you must take a stand.

Demand that your siblings help. If they live out of town and that's their built-in excuse for not lending a hand, ask them to send you some money so that you can hire an aide once a week. Use that time to be with friends. If your siblings complain, push back. Loneliness is taking a toll on your life. Explain the sacrifices you've been making. You might even make a list. Detail the errands you're running and the meals you're prepping. Since they don't see all the work you're doing, there's a chance they don't know.

If being overly generous with your time is making you miserable, it's time to be selfish. And let's face it, if your siblings have dumped the entire load of caregiving on your back—the scheduling of doctors' appointments, the overseeing of home repairs—then they've been acting selfishly all along.

Invest in Your Body

You might be shocked to learn, since I am known for talking about sex, that for many years, on and off, my husband Fred and I slept in separate beds. (He snored!) Please don't worry: We found many other places and times to be intimate. But I am a more patient person and generally a much happier person when I get enough rest, and because of that, Fred and I made the joint decision that sleeping apart from time to time was worth it for both of us.

Sleep has always been important to me. One of the hardest aspects of getting back to my normal and busy routine after I had a stroke in 2023, and another minor one this year, was all the trouble I had falling asleep and staying asleep. When it was finally morning and time to begin my day, I was often too tired to do all the talking and planning I wanted to do. I worked with my doctors, changing a few poststroke medications, to get my sleeping routine back on track.

My situation didn't get better immediately, and while that was incredibly frustrating to me, it slowly improved. I was soon able to see friends again, visit with family, and finish writing this book!

I want you to think about how much sleep you're getting. And while you're at it, think about how well you're eating and how much exercise you're getting. If you are not prioritizing rest, if you are not investing in your body, you likely won't have the interest or stamina to engage with other people, and interacting with other people is the only way to create and maintain meaningful connections.

Indulge Yourself

The absence of human touch can be especially painful. Most people crave physical connection—a warm embrace, a thoughtful squeeze on the shoulder—so when we don't have it, we can feel even more isolated. From the moment we are born, skin-to-skin touch contributes to our physical development and mental health. It's been proven to fight disease, help us feel more relaxed, and make us less depressed.

If you're lonely, you may not have the opportunity to be touched very often. One way to counter this vacuum, at least until you develop more intimate relationships, is to treat yourself to manicures, pedicures, and massages. Or get even more creative and go to an acupuncturist. There's no right or wrong number of times to go—indulging every now and then is a chance to feel a sense of physical connection.

When I first hit it big, I bought a massage table and hired a masseuse to come to my apartment once a week. Everyone who worked for me knew I was not available during that time. I was enjoying myself. I was recharging my batteries. I looked forward to being rubbed all over!

By the way, it's possible to enjoy the benefits of massage without spending any money at all. Research at the University of Miami School of Medicine shows that self-massage—rubbing your own arms and legs—also provides positive effects. Why not give it a shot?

Master the Art of Masturbation

Here's a word you might not have expected to find in a book on loneliness, though it may be a little less surprising since it's one of my books: *masturbation*. Being lonely doesn't have to include feeling sexually frustrated.

If you don't have a partner, you should feel free to indulge in some guilt-free masturbation. Be aware, however, that I used the word *some*. As with many other pleasure-inducing activities, too much masturbation—like too many potato chips—can become a problem.

If you're routinely canceling plans so you can stay home to pleasure yourself, that's a warning sign of excessive masturbation. And if you're masturbating every single day, then I say it's likely part of the reason you are lonely.

Frequently reaching climax on your own removes one of the most important incentives for finding a sexual partner. You have to place a limit on how often you engage in this activity. I want your desire for arousal to motivate your search for a healthy sexual relationship. Your longing for intimacy has the capacity to force you out the door, but only if you let it. And that's what I want for you.

Embrace Your Inner Turtle

Making new connections requires courage. If you're shy or lack confidence, if you're an introvert, it can be especially uncomfortable and intimidating to put yourself into social situations. A good remedy for being timid is to embrace your inner turtle.

When a turtle pulls its head and legs inside its shell, it's safe. Nothing can hurt it, but eventually the turtle must stick its neck out. A turtle can't hunt for food, bask in the sun, or find a mate if it plays it safe forever. Turtles must take risks in order to live. The symbolism has always inspired me, and it's why I have an enormous collection of miniature turtles in my apartment. I literally have hundreds. Blue. Yellow. Pink. Red. Rainbow-colored. Green. Most are enameled and covered in rhinestones and imitation gems. They line nearly every one of my bookshelves. There are so many on my living room coffee table, there's no longer room to put my cup of coffee. (Lest you think I've gone off the deep end, most of these turtles were gifts and my collection never seems to stop growing!)

At this point maybe you're assuming, because I have so many turtles, that I never have a problem coming out of my shell. Maybe you're under the impression that it's always been easy for me to talk in front of audiences and deliver speeches. It certainly became easier over the years, especially since I taught sex education in front of hundreds of college students at a time, but I still feel butterflies in my stomach standing in front of a crowd. But I push myself. And you should, too.

I recognize that sometimes even speaking with one person might feel like the scariest stage ever. If that's how it feels to you, if you find yourself frequently staying inside your shell, don't forget to engage your inner turtle. It might help you grow a smidge braver, like it has for me.

Bring a Prop

When my book *Sex for Dummies* was published, the marketing people were very clever with how they promoted the book. They produced keepsake key chains, tiny replicas of the famous bright yellow cover. I don't remember how many I was given to pass out at events, but I am sure I exceeded whatever number they budgeted for. Readers loved them, many asked for extras to give to friends, and I requested more and more to give away.

Looking back, I don't think the key chains were popular simply because they were free. Sure, that was part of it, but I believe people wanted them because they made it easier to approach me. Those little plastic rectangles were conversation starters. Readers who might have been uncomfortable coming up to me otherwise had an easy way to begin talking to me—to ask for a key chain.

Since you probably don't have a key chain with your name on it, how can you make it more likely for someone to walk up to you? What can you do to appear more friendly and open to a conversation?

Think visually.

Put on a T-shirt with the name of your high school or college. Wear a hat with your favorite sport team's logo. Bring a bestselling book to a coffee shop and read it for a while, making sure the cover is visible to anyone who walks by. If you need to get some work done, that's OK. Place a few stickers on your laptop. Choose organizations you support, singers and bands you like, or mountains you've climbed. Welcome any conversations that naturally unfold.

A carefully chosen prop can signal your interests and affiliations. Without saying a word, you've made it easier for like-minded individuals to initiate a conversation with you. And who knows? These shared connections may lead to deeper discussions and potentially the formation of new friendships. (I hope you're realizing by now that I'm urging you to take very small steps in your battle against loneliness. Small steps are important because they're more doable and sustainable than larger ones. Over time, they'll add up and you'll be happier and have more connections!)

Get a Dog

There's no better loneliness-beating pet than a dog. Sure, all pets offer wonders for your psyche. And yes, I do understand cats are cuddly. But for the purposes of this loneliness conversation we're having, animals that you mostly enjoy in solitude won't help you find new human companionship. This is why having a dog is a better option for anyone who is lonely.

Dogs are the most popular pet in the United States, and because of that dogs are people magnets. A dog is your ticket to meet other dog owners at a dog run. A dog is your excuse to go for a walk, multiple times a day, and chat with your neighbors. If you're not comfortable making small talk, dogs can help. A sweet, adorable dog may be just the kind of icebreaker you need!

But let's be clear: Dogs are a lot of work. I wouldn't want you to get one without giving the idea of dog ownership a lot of thought. Learn about the different breeds and what each brings to the table in terms of care and personality. Take into account your own physical abilities. You don't want to get a big and jumpy dog if you're on the frail side. You don't want to get an animal for emotional support only to wind up unable to handle the physical stress and responsibility.

Practice Small Kindnesses

It's a good idea while we're still at the beginning of this book to set the record straight. I've focused so far on the many ways little steps can lead to establishing new and meaningful relationships. But let's pause for a moment. Loneliness is not only about the absence of good friends and sexual partners. Loneliness may stem from not feeling connected much to anyone.

Research shows that if you strike up even the briefest of conversations with a stranger, both of you will feel better and more connected. Asking the person standing next to you in an elevator how their day is going invites conversation. Picking up a piece of mail your neighbor dropped and handing it over with a kind word and a smile sparks discussion. As authors Ryan Jenkins and Steven Van Cohen say in their book *Connectable,* connections don't have to be lasting to be meaningful.

When my daughter, Miriam, was getting married, the best place to shop for wedding dresses was a store in Bay Ridge, Brooklyn, the same New York City neighborhood where Pierre lives. Miriam and I took a car service to the store and looked through every rack for a gown, and then I asked the driver to take us to visit Pierre and his family. I'd never met this driver before, but rather than let him wait in the car for us, I invited him inside. Later, Miriam asked whether the driver was someone I'd hired many times before, but, in fact, it was the first time. Looking back, we all felt very good meeting someone new that day!

Being comfortable talking with people you don't know is a skill. It will take time and practice, like getting better at swimming or playing the piano. I wish there were a magic button that you could push and—shazam!—you'd no longer be lonely. Unfortunately there isn't. There are no shortcuts. But if you make the conscious decision to interact with strangers, and force yourself to do so regularly, it will enhance feelings of connection to the world around you. And the more you do it, the easier it will get.

Push Through Rejection

Fear of being rejected is what holds many people back from making connections. I understand that. Rejection is hard to take. It makes you sad, angry, and confused, sometimes all at once. The problem is that rejection is a part of the human experience. I don't want you to take it too personally. You can't avoid it, and it's hardly ever within your control. Certainly, I don't want you to end your quest for new or deeper relationships because you're worried about being rejected again. (My guess is that your luck will change.)

I want you to have only one reaction to rejection: Lick your wounds and try again. The companions you make along the way will more than make up for those who pushed you aside.

Learn the Westheimer Maneuver

One tried-and-true method of meeting new people is to take classes. Now, if your main reason for signing up for a course like painting or Italian cooking is to learn a new hobby, then I'd say sign up for a beginner's class. But since your main goal is to forge new connections, I suggest a different tactic. Yes, sign up for a beginner's class, but pick a course where you already have some expertise!

Why would you do that, you ask? If you're already somewhat skilled, you'll have a leg up on everyone else. If the person next to you is having trouble, you can grin and say, "Here, let me help you with that." Your confidence will soar! And making friends will be so much easier with this newfound well of self-assurance.

I call this approach the Westheimer Maneuver. It's making the decision to be audacious—to do mostly whatever it takes to get what you want. I'll give you an example of how I've put the Westheimer Maneuver into action.

A few years ago, I was about to debate a woman at the Oxford Union, a distinguished debating society in England, about pornography being part of sex education in schools. (I was arguing that porn, if talked about appropriately, should be discussed; she was claiming that it had no place in the classroom.) The Oxford Union is probably the most prestigious site where debates are held, and I was nervous. At the dinner before the event that evening, I noticed that whenever someone proposed a toast, my opponent always took a considerable gulp of wine. I, on the other hand, barely let the wine touch my lips. So I began to chime in. I proposed toast after toast, and the result was that I won the debate easily. You can't be a good debater if you're tipsy!

Taking advantage of circumstances is hardly a new idea. Back in the day, many a lady "accidentally" dropped her handkerchief in front of some man she wanted to meet. Using situations to your advantage, only if it does no harm, isn't trickery—it's chutzpah!

Turn Lemons into Lemonade

My late husband Fred and I met because I refused to accept a less-than-ideal situation. It wasn't a life-or-death predicament, not by a long shot, but I did make an important decision that turned an uncomfortable situation upside down. If I hadn't taken action, my life would be very different today.

Let me tell you what happened.

I've always loved downhill skiing, and one day in 1961 I hit the slopes with three friends because one of them belonged to a ski club and the group had planned a weekend getaway. My ski partner and I were a disaster right from the start. To get to the top of the ski run, we had to use a T-bar—a metal bar skiers put under their tushes to pull them up the mountain. Let me just say that the system works well if two people are similar in height. But for a mismatched pair like us—my friend was more than six feet tall—the mechanism was awkward and difficult to use. When the bar was under *his* tush, it was at my neck; when it was under *my* tush, the bar was at his ankles.

We fumbled and had many false starts. When we finally got to the top, I was so frustrated that I skied off to the side. That's when I spotted Fred. Fred was president of the ski club that my other friend belonged to. Fred was not very tall. Without hesitation, I said to my tall friend: "From now on I'm going up the mountain with that short guy." And that's exactly what Fred and I did.

My decision was abrupt, may even have been rude to my tall friend, but my choice to change ski partners salvaged my day of skiing. It also set me on a new path that opened up other opportunities and possibilities.

There's a saying: When life gives you lemons, make lemonade. If you run into a situation where difficulties make it impossible for you to succeed, don't throw your hands up and cry uncle. Scan your surroundings. Find a solution. Optimists are always more attractive than pessimists. Once you discover a work-around, squeeze your lemon hard and never look back.

Prepare for Conversation

David Letterman had me on his show many times, and I always loved it. On one occasion, the producers came up with a twist: The studio audience would choose nearly everything that unfolded. By the sound of applause, the crowd decided what Dave wore, the theme music to begin the program, and who should read the opening announcements. The routine was hilarious. And then, while the audience was still in a tizzy, Dave asked which of two guests he should bring out first. The choice was between Teri Garr (nominated for an Academy Award for *Tootsie* and one of the stars in Steven Spielberg's *Close Encounters of the Third Kind*) and me. I immediately felt sorry for Teri. Even though she was a lot more attractive than me and a very accomplished actor, my subject matter (sex!) was certain to win the day, and it did.

The lesson here is that when it comes to connecting with people, the ability to be entertaining is key. Have something unusual or provocative to say! Don't be the person who only complains. Don't be the person who always brags about their kids. And never go into a social situation without an idea or two of how you can be interesting.

Pick subjects that are a little off the beaten path yet intriguing to most people. (Stay away from the latest headlines or what's trending on social media, because everyone will probably know about them already.) When there's a lull in conversation, you can break in with "Did you hear . . ." I guarantee you'll have a spot in whatever discussion develops. And be prepared for questions! By digging into your topic just a little bit, you'll be more able to keep the conversation going.

Being curious about people is also a great way to get conversations going. Need suggestions? Here are two from newspaper columnist David Brooks, author of *How to Know a Person: The Art of Seeing Others Deeply and Being Deeply Seen*:

> "Where did you grow up?" (Most people enjoy talking about their childhood, so this is a great one!)
>
> "What's your favorite unimportant thing about you?" (David says he likes early Taylor Swift even better than later Taylor Swift. David is known as a serious journalist, so this would be fun to discuss with him at a party!) No matter the questions you ask, he says the goal is the same: to get people talking and telling stories.

And what if you're an introvert? I say practice what you're going to say and give yourself ample time to rest and recharge after you leave any kind of big social event. Introverts aren't necessarily shy, but being in large group settings can be exhausting for them. Instead of drawing energy from people, like I do, introverts tire from external stimulation. If this describes you, know this about yourself and plan time to unwind and regroup after you've gone out for the evening. And while you may not be prepping to go on late-night television, know that everyone who speaks professionally rehearses what they're going to say. So should you.

Don't Hide Who You Are

My first language is German, and I learned Hebrew when I moved to Palestine (before the establishment of Israel) and then French when I lived as a student in Paris. In 1956, when I arrived in the United States, I spoke very little English, and like so many immigrants, I had an accent. My accent identified me as German, and well-meaning friends thought I should take elocution lessons, urging me to modify my accent or get rid of it altogether. (After the war, there was still a lot of anti-German sentiment in New York and other places, and they were concerned for my safety.) But I didn't have the time or money for that, and looking back, I'm glad. My accent is what made me recognizable on the radio. My accent helped make me famous.

If you're an immigrant, I imagine you're trying to fit in as you settle into your new surroundings. But there's no need to go overboard. Don't be ashamed of your accent or your clothing or whatever it is that makes you unique. In fact, use these differences to make friends. When you meet someone new, smile widely and say something like "You understand me despite my accent, right?" This will hopefully start a positive discussion about where you're from and how you got here, and anytime you can start a conversation, you have the opportunity to create a new connection. And if someone clearly doesn't want to be friends with you, no matter the reason, just move on.

And here's one more story about my unique way of talking that you just can't make up: You know what Debra Jo Rupp, the actress who starred in *That '70s Show,* had to do when she played me in Mark St. Germain's play *Becoming Dr. Ruth*? Take lessons on how to speak with *my* accent! How ironic is that?

Travel Wisely

It matters where you sleep when you're on vacation. Yes, I love a big hotel as much as the next person, and my favorite is the King David Hotel in Jerusalem. It has everything I could ever want—a gorgeous outdoor pool, a great view of the city, and plenty of places to sit outside and get a bite to eat. What it doesn't have are ready-made conversation partners. Unless you ask the concierge a question, you could go days without talking with another human being.

This is why I think hostels and especially bed-and-breakfasts are the best accommodations for people who are lonely.

Innkeepers are the perfect hosts. They want to make you feel at home because in most cases where you're staying is their home. Without your having to ask a question, owners recommend what to do and what to see during your visit. And for breakfast, instead of seating you in a cavernous room where guests tend to stick to themselves, they'll show you to a table in a small space with very few other guests, where conversations are far more likely to happen. Perhaps you'll decide to check out the local museum with another solo traveler.

Choose Mental Wealth

I grew up in Frankfurt. Before the Nazis came to power, it was a wonderful place to be a child. My neighborhood was idyllic. It seemed that I knew every neighbor and that my parents always had an extra pair of hands to take me to the store or walk me to school.

For some people, especially those in the United States who are college-educated, it's common these days to move a great distance because of work. A new job across the country might offer a better job title and salary. But uprooting yourself from childhood friends and family comes at a cost.

What happens if you decide a decade or so after you

move to start a family? If you're three thousand miles away from your parents, you won't have that ready-made support system. You might feel increasingly alone and isolated. The same would be true if you needed ongoing help after breaking your leg or managing a chronic illness. When life is hard, it might be easier if you're surrounded by people who've known and loved you for a lifetime. (It will also be easier to care for aging parents—and feel more connected to them—if you don't live in a different time zone.)

I urge you to prioritize your mental (not just financial) wealth. Yes, I know that money is important and that I am writing from a place where I haven't struggled to pay my bills for a long time, but try not to make work the only factor when considering where to live. My advice is to think about how your everyday existence might look years from now when your lifestyle and needs change.

Communicate Your Needs

You should always tell people what you need, and that's especially true if you're grieving. Loneliness increases when you feel the people closest to you aren't supporting you or don't understand what you're going through. But let's not assume the worst of them. They may have zero experience with loss, and they're certainly not mind readers. Unless you tell people how they can show up for you, how should they know?

My co-author Allison is a journalist, and she writes a lot about grief. If you're feeling alone because nobody remembered to call you on the anniversary of your loved one's death, Allison advises that you ask at least one person to mark the date on their calendar so that *next year* you're assured a phone call.

I've always told my radio listeners and TV watchers to communicate their wishes in the bedroom. If you like to be stimulated a certain way, you need to tell your lover what to do! If you like oral sex, you should ask your partner for more oral sex! This kind of directness is important at all times in your life, and that includes times of great sadness. Communicating your needs will help your needs be met, and when your needs are met, you will feel less lonely. This is uniquely true when dealing with family, and that's precisely why we're going to focus on family relationships next.

Family

FAMILY PLAYS AN ESSENTIAL ROLE IN REDUCING loneliness. When relationships are possible, family members provide a unique and powerful sense of belonging and understanding. They also contribute a feeling of security, a go-to support system, so much so that it's possible you might never experience the sensation of being completely alone. And because family relationships are so vital for social connection, doing whatever you can to preserve, repair, and strengthen these bonds should be a priority.

Of course, not all family situations are positive, I realize, and I recognize that the absence of family connections can feel incredibly isolating. You likely grew up with the understanding that family is supposed to have your back no matter what—so that when you no longer have access to that kind of unconditional love and support, you may feel particularly empty. I also know, because I lost my family so young, that death can be a significant cause of loneliness. I tried to stay in touch with my family after we were separated. We wrote letters back and forth for a time, but then my letters stopped being answered. I longed for family so much and for so long that I eventually built myself a new one from scratch.

This portion of the Menu for Connection is about rebuilding connections with family—whether you're estranged, separated by loss, or just living far away.

The American Psychological Association defines loneliness as "discomfort or uneasiness from being or perceiving oneself to be alone." Pay close attention to just one of these words: *perceiving*.

How lonely you feel depends on how you *perceive* your circumstances. If you think you are powerless, then you are likely going to feel worse. But here I am. I'm telling you that it's possible to mend relationships with parents and siblings, build an entirely new family when your birth family no longer exists, rekindle a relationship with an estranged family member, and even maintain close relationships with family members who are no longer alive. (In cases of physical and mental abuse, it may be safest and more empowering to focus on creating new family-type connections instead.)

Follow my advice. When you put effort into strengthening family connections, your life can change. It can become richer and fuller. My bet is that you'll also be happier.

Rethink Your Thinking

If you're lucky, family offers a safe harbor from the world. You feel accepted into the group, like you belong, no matter what. Shared history, traditions, and values create this kind of powerful connection. And yet family can easily be torn apart. And not just by what we say or do but also by how we think. I am sure you know that our mind, in many ways, controls our actions. Negative thinking often brings more negativity into our lives. Positive thinking, you guessed it, frequently brings more positivity into our lives.

I believe you can mend nearly any hurt just by changing the way you think. Mind over matter. Even if we can't change our circumstances (maybe you and your family member are no longer speaking to each other), we can change the way we view those circumstances. Pushing ourselves to believe that one day we'll see a brighter tomorrow opens us up to the possibility that life won't always be so bleak and that we'll be able to repair nearly any family relationship.

I learned this lesson when I was ten years old.

When my father was taken away by the Nazis, I was in our apartment in Frankfurt. I remember watching from the window as he was led into a truck. He looked up at me and smiled. I've never forgotten the reassuring expression on his face. I'm sure he wasn't in the mood to smile. He must have feared what might happen to him next, what would happen to me, his only child. But his decision to smile in that dreadful moment made me hopeful.

When my mother and grandmother put me on a train to Switzerland a few weeks later, part of the Kindertransport to save the lives of Jewish children, I made sure my grandmother and mother saw me smiling out the window when the train left the station. I was terrified and had no idea if I would ever see my parents and grandmother again, but I did what I could to make them feel better, just as my father had done for me.

Sometime on the journey, as improbable as it sounds, I stood on my seat and started to sing the Hebrew songs we all were taught in school. I sang as loudly as I could. The other children soon joined me, and for the rest of the ride, there was no crying, only singing.

To patch relationships with family members, you might need to fake a smile until a real smile emerges. You might need to forgive or forget. And you might need to change your mindset—to believe that a relationship is fixable and not broken forever. You'll be more likely to rebuild fractured relationships because you'll be pushing yourself to look at bad situations with a little more optimism.

By the way, I learned something else on that train. I began to understand how wonderful it feels to make others feel better. I have no idea if I made my mother and grandmother feel better when they saw me smile out the window, but I was trying to give them hope, like my father had given me. And while I didn't have any family with me on that train, I did have one companion: my favorite doll. There was a little girl half my age sitting next to me. She was crying even harder than I was. So what did I do? I gave her my doll. These were the germs of my becoming a therapist, of my realizing I had the power to make people feel better.

Go to Gatherings

Push yourself to attend weddings, graduations, confirmations, quinceañeras—any gathering where family is involved. Don't allow your distaste for any one aunt or uncle, niece or nephew, to keep you away. The lonelier you are, the more you need your family. If you hide yourself away every time your family assembles, you're cutting yourself off from building on the relationships you do enjoy. But the scenario can also play out much worse than this.

If you always skip family events, if you always come up with some excuse for why it isn't possible for you to go, pretty soon they'll begin to write you off and you won't be invited at all. You may end up with no baby showers and no retirement parties to celebrate.

Yes, I know it can be unpleasant to have to grin while some relative fills your ear with comments you despise. But keep in mind that family events are social events, and you can move around as if you're at a cocktail party—moving from one conversation to the next, not spending too long with anyone.

Be Less Judgmental

Everyone experiences loneliness, but because you are reading this book, it seems you are maybe feeling lonelier than most. This is a clue that you're not perfect. You, like the rest of us, have flaws.

Why do I bring this up?

Because undoubtedly you have family members who also have imperfections. Are they annoying because they talk incessantly? Do they irritate you because they think they're smarter than you? Whatever your grievance, since you also are not perfect, and because you're feeling disconnected, you have to find a way to make peace with them and fold them into your life.

Ignore what irks you. Bite your tongue. Hold your breath. Suck on a mint. Drink tea. Or make a decision to lean into it and adapt—instead of throwing away the relationship.

If your aunt always goes on and on about the same topic, the next time you see her, come prepared with questions about another subject so you can redirect the conversation. If your grandmother can't hear very well and you hate having to shout, make a point of not talking so much and simply hold her hand. I promise you she'll like it, and you'll both feel less lonely.

By the way, I'm not shy about asking friends and relatives to hold my hand. It's a way of communicating that works for me no matter how sad, frustrated, or tired I might feel. Touch is powerful. Without saying a word, it can help us feel less alone.

Admit Your Mistakes

In late 1985 and early 1986, I was caught up in a rather large controversy. It began when a librarian in Ramsey, New Jersey, reached out to my publisher to complain about my book *First Love*. She told my editor that, effective immediately, it was being removed from circulation. No, the book wasn't being banned. It wasn't too explicit. The problem was a small yet significant typo.

In a passage about reducing the risk of pregnancy, I wrote that it's safe to have sex the week before and the week of ovulation. But that's incorrect. The word *safe* should have been *unsafe*. The publisher recalled 115,000 copies of the book, we added those two all-important letters, and it was rereleased with an entirely new cover. I don't know how that mistake wound up in the book, as I certainly knew the correct information, but I didn't hesitate to take full responsibility. My name was on the book, so it was my fault.

How are you at admitting your mistakes? Your refusal to say "I'm sorry" could be one of the reasons your family relationships have suffered. It might also be one of the reasons you're lonely. To resuscitate these connections, you may need to swallow your pride. You may need to extend that apology, even if it should have been offered years ago. When you acknowledge wrongdoing, you are better positioned to get family relationships back on track.

Even if your fumbles don't make national headlines (my error was covered by nearly every newspaper and magazine in America), it's never too late to make things right. Keep your ego in check. Don't let it cause any more distance and pain.

Channel Your Inner Shark

Having thick skin is important for keeping and nurturing family relationships because if you can't take a joke, if your feathers get ruffled too easily, you might as well decide that being lonely isn't so bad after all. You might have a rude stepfather. Your mother's politics may offend you. You have to learn to look the other way. You have to develop the thickest skin of anyone you know. The whale shark has one of the thickest skins of any animal in the world. To keep family connections close, you must channel your inner shark!

I kept my mouth shut plenty of times with Fred's relatives. Some were less than thrilled when he told them we were getting married. I was not the catch they were hoping for. I was a single mother, and they didn't think I was good enough for him. From the moment Fred reported this back to me, I had to smile and be friendly whenever I saw them, all the while knowing they were against our marriage. Over the years, my attitude toward them softened. They were loving toward me, and I adored them. If I had held on to my anger, we all would have missed out.

If someone is inconsiderate, let it go. If it happens again and again, address the problem directly. Make sure tension doesn't build and emotional wounds don't fester. And if you learn family members are talking about you behind your back, it might be best to think about whale sharks and just keep your lips closed.

Be a Good Listener

I mentioned on page 28 that when I first stepped foot in the United States I barely spoke English. I knew how to exchange a few pleasantries, but as a refugee, I found it challenging to navigate New York and start over again. My lifeline was a German Jewish newspaper called the *Aufbau*. Reading the paper one day, I spotted an ad that would change my life: The New School of Social Research was offering a scholarship for a master's degree in sociology. Only victims of the Nazis could apply. The next day I went to the school, and twenty-four hours later I got the scholarship. The New School is where I met Hannah Strauss, who quickly became my best friend.

Hannah—more than anyone else before or since—taught me one of the most valuable lessons in maintaining deep connections: Be a good listener. Hannah seemed to appreciate whatever I had to say. Whenever we talked, I felt like all of her attention was on me. She never brushed aside my troubles, and she always wanted to hear my good news. By actively listening, by giving me her unrushed and undivided focus, Hannah made me feel important, and that good feeling made me like her even more. When I became a therapist, I tried my best to copy Hannah's way of being. In my private practice, I wanted to be the best listener I could be and help my clients arrive at their own solutions. On my radio show, I wanted callers to know that their concerns were valid and that I wouldn't judge them for asking a question.

When you listen, you can't talk, and when you don't talk, you can't come across as a know-it-all. You also can't make people feel stupid for their indecision or actions. Family members will feel closer to you, and your relationships will deepen, when you acknowledge their worries but don't chime in every chance you get with your opinions. Sit with your child's problems and don't be ready to fix them so quickly.

Families often experience rifts when there's too much talking and not enough listening. The next time you want to offer some unsolicited advice, I hope you'll think about Hannah. Open your ears and close your mouth as much as possible.

Be Vulnerable

I come from a long line of German Jews who don't typically complain. My family always thought it best to be stoic. And while to some extent I remain this way, it's no longer possible to completely keep my problems to myself. Today, because of my age, I've come to accept there are some challenges that I can't solve on my own. I tell my daughter, Miriam, and my son, Joel, everything that involves my healthcare, and they make sure I have the help I need to safely navigate my apartment. It wasn't easy admitting that I needed help. It wasn't in my nature to accept assistance or show weakness. In many ways, looking back on my life now, I should have leaned on others more frequently than I did. Doing so certainly would have made being a young working mother easier.

I want you to learn from my experiences and ask for more support. Please don't take this to mean that I advocate hanging a sign around your neck that declares "I'm lonely" and walking around your neighborhood. What I want you to do is appoint your own personal ambassador to loneliness. Reach out to at least one family member and tell that one person the truth about how you're feeling. Perhaps a cousin, aunt, or grandparent can play this role. Confide in that one person. Give your ambassador permission to tell others in your family that you'd welcome more texts, phone calls, and visits.

Loneliness is invisible. You might put on such a

good front that nobody in your family is even aware that you're lonely. If you don't admit you need help, help may never come.

Say Their Name Out Loud

There are many reasons why families no longer talk about one family member or another. Death. Prison. Divorce. Drugs. Estrangement for any reason. Abuse of any kind. While you can't bring a loved one back from the dead, and you can't unilaterally shift perceptions of the black sheep of the family, you can determine what you do and what you say in any given situation.

Tell stories about your sister, brother, mother, or father—even if no one else does. Bring their name up in conversation. You can be the one person in your family who acknowledges a birthday or the anniversary of a death.

Ignoring that there was an important person in your family and feeling that you're the only person who still remembers or cares can make you feel especially alone and disconnected. That's loneliness on top of loneliness—you're missing your loved one and you're not able to talk about your loved one. To beat back loneliness, say the name of your missing family member out loud. Do this whenever the moment moves you, at any time you crave a sense of connection.

Fabricate an Excuse

If you no longer speak with members of your family simply because too much time has passed, you might benefit from creating an excuse to get back in touch. Sure, you could just start by calling cousins out of the blue, but that might feel awkward. A perfectly acceptable reason to get back in touch is to get their help with a genealogy project. If you're not researching your family tree or writing up your family's history, it's time to get started. Get started right now!

Your first phone call is simply to invite them to lend a hand. If relatives happen to live nearby, make a point of saying, "Let's make a plan to look at photographs together." Of course, if meeting one-on-one feels strange, you could try to piece together a small group of relatives instead. A gathering would allow everyone to share memories, and I bet each person who participates will feel a surge of meaningful connection, most of all *you*—since you're the one who did all the planning to make it happen.

If creating a video is more your style, you could ask relatives to sit down with you for interviews. I've made several documentaries, two as a producer and one that I starred in called *Ask Dr. Ruth,* by the director Ryan White. You may not see yourself as a documentary filmmaker, but I suggest you begin rethinking that. Working on a film is fun. It also has the capacity to bring family back into your life. But no matter what kind of genealogy project you choose, a shared endeavor is a perfect way to mend or rekindle familial relationships.

Have Family Game Night

Even if you have a great relationship with your spouse and children, the everyday demands of raising a family can make you feel more like a short-order cook than a parent who is seen, valued, and loved. Feeling unnoticed and unappreciated is not a good recipe for feeling connected to family. In fact, a root cause of loneliness is being surrounded by people who you expect will make you feel whole but instead make you feel like part of the furniture.

Family game nights can help. For a few hours, the whole family can play with one another and not worry about chores, to-do lists, or homework. Children see their parents as playmates, not taskmasters. Remembering to take time out to play can make everyone feel closer and more connected.

When I started to become more famous, I was asked to endorse many products. I rejected most of these offers, because the advice I was giving was important and I didn't want people to think I was some sort of huckster. I wanted to be known as a trained expert, and I wanted my advice to be trusted. But I did agree to having one board game with my name on it—Dr. Ruth's Game of Good Sex. I considered it a great way to deliver valuable sex education to an even wider audience. And while I would never recommend it for family game night (it's not at all appropriate for children!), I do suggest competing against one another with games like Apples to Apples and Ticket to Ride or classics like Clue or the great card game euchre.

In an unexpected way, working on Dr. Ruth's Game of Good Sex made me feel closer to my parents. When the venture was just taking off, I needed to pick a name for my company. I chose Karola Inc. in recognition of my birth name, Karola. When I immigrated to Israel, I was told Karola sounded too German and that I should change it. I decided to flip my first and middle names. My middle name, Ruth, became my first name. My first name, Karola, became my middle name.

I had been fearful of getting rid of Karola altogether. If there was any chance my mother and father had survived the concentration camps and were looking for me, I needed them to see Karola associated with my name. Sadly, even though my dream never came true, looking back now, choosing to name my company Karola Inc. strengthened my relationship with them. It renewed my sense of connection to my parents.

Share the Fun

I've always loved playing chess. As soon as my grandchildren were old enough, I took out my chessboard and we'd compete. Pitting your wits against one another—no matter the game you choose—is a fantastic bonding opportunity. And before you argue, "But my grandchildren live too far away," you can still play games even if they live in another state or country.

The New York Times is my favorite newspaper and has some of the best games for nurturing family relationships. Wordle, Connections, and The Mini Crossword are all great ones to try. What's terrific about them is that everyone plays the same game on the same day—offering a consistent way to stay in touch no matter the distance. And because players can easily share their results with one another via text, I know many parents who play with their college-age kids, too. For them, it's an easy and enjoyable way to stay in touch throughout the academic year.

Sharing scores and bragging rights isn't serious—but the benefits of all that reliable social interaction are. After all, maintaining connections is easier when we can share experiences.

Lose Count

When Miriam was a baby and I was a single mother, I had no money for a babysitter in order to go out with family or friends. My solution was to throw parties in my apartment. The remedy was so simple and successful that I continued to host gatherings in my living room long after Miriam was an adult. Larry Angelo, my wonderful cohost on Lifetime's *Good Sex, with Dr. Ruth Westheimer* and other TV shows, remembers them well. "Everyone brought things to eat and drink and you'd call them 'Bring Something' parties," he fondly recalled as we reminisced for this book. Time and time again I'd offer up my home. I made myself a perpetual hostess.

If you're always the one initiating plans, whether to organize a small gathering or a large family reunion, it's easy to get resentful and say "Enough." I understand the desire to count how many times your invitations go unreciprocated. But I encourage you to change your thinking: Your payback isn't a future dinner at your relative's house. Your payback is having the opportunity to strengthen your connections right now, on your own timetable.

We can never understand what's going on behind a relative's closed doors. Maybe your cousin is self-conscious about her home. Perhaps the expense of hosting (providing drinks and anything else) feels a bit too much. At the end of the day, decide to be a host because it makes you feel less isolated. Don't even think about being invited anywhere ever. Try to focus on the upside—having relatives to spend time with and enjoying their company.

Be a Team Player–Literally

In my therapy practice, I saw clients with many different kinds of sexual problems. Couples who lost interest in sex were very common. What was also common was *why* they had lost interest in sex. Frequently they had fallen into a pattern of feeling disconnected from each other. Even though they were living under the same roof, going to sleep and waking up in the same bed, they felt lonely. Perhaps lonelier than if they were single, because they had unmet expectations of feeling close and connected.

To get back on track, think outside the bedroom and consider what fun activities you could do with your partner. Relationships frequently suffer when couples stop doing stuff together. Pickleball is typically played in pairs. Two people are on each side of the net at all times. I love the idea of you and your partner forming a team together. I also happen to love dancing. Dancing—in particular ballroom, salsa, foxtrot, and more—requires that you rely on your partner and operate in unison. It also demands plenty of touching, always a good thing for couples!

Physical activity has the power to rebuild emotional intimacy. When you play a sport together, you must work collaboratively to win. When you dance, you have to clasp hands and thrust your pelvis into your partner's hips. Physical closeness and synchronized movement have the power to enhance emotional bonds. They also create shared memories, enabling couples to deepen their connection even further.

Grow Independently

Please don't take my previous point to mean that you have to spend every free second with your partner to feel connected. The secret is finding a healthy blend of time together and time apart. Somewhere in the middle is where you will feel full and complete. Somewhere in the middle is where you'll recognize yourself and feel like you belong in your own home.

When I married Fred, my third husband, he already had a paramour: a plot of land he owned on Lake Oscawana in Putnam Valley, New York. He loved nothing more than spending time there—with or without me. The kids and I enjoyed the water, but if I had something else to do (and my travel schedule was quite hectic for years), I'd routinely take a pass. But truthfully, that didn't upset him. He was more than happy to go alone. If he'd been stuck in our Washington Heights apartment with no companion, I'm sure he would have resented my going off all the time. And if I had put my work on the back burner just to accommodate him, I would have felt angry and diminished.

Going in different directions can fortify relationships. Once we shelve what's most important to us, once we start making so many compromises we lose our sense of self, that's when loneliness bubbles up. Don't accept a bad situation. Talk it out with your spouse or partner. There's more to life than wallowing in misery.

Set a New Course

If your misery is unshakable no matter how many activities you try with and without your partner, you might be better off ending your relationship and starting fresh. Believe me, I know what I'm talking about. I've been in three marriages. I mentioned already that my beloved Fred was my third husband. What I haven't told you yet is anything about the other two.

David (pronounced Dah-VEED) was my first husband. We met through mutual friends when I was teaching kindergarten in Israel. He was smart and handsome. Even better, he was short and a good dancer! I fell for David immediately and we were engaged and married all within a few months.

What a mess it turned out to be. We married too young and grew apart.

I met Dan after David. By this time, I was living in Paris, and we decided to leave France and head to the United States. We weren't married, but when we arrived in New York, we found an apartment together through that newspaper I told you about, the *Aufbau*. Then I got pregnant by accident. And then we got married. Miriam was born one year after I arrived in America, but even Miriam, this gorgeous and perfect baby, couldn't make our marriage last.

Dan and I realized we weren't right for each other. As with my marriage to David, if Dan and I had forced ourselves to stay together, I would have been miserable and lonely. He wasn't the right partner for me, and he would never become the right partner, even if we had spent eternity side by side.

Have you and your partner drifted in different directions, too? Might counseling repair your relationship? Possibly. Therapists aren't magicians, though, and if a relationship needs to end, the sooner you make the split the better. And even though personal finances may make some situations more complicated than others, my hope is that you'll find your way to another partner—one who will make you feel happier and more complete. As long as your spirit is free to soar, you'll have the freedom to get to know yourself again and develop a new and far more fulfilling romantic relationship.

Preserve In-law Relationships

Dan didn't have family, but David did, and after David and I divorced, I made sure to stay in touch. As you know, I lost my mother, father, and grandparents during the Holocaust, and other than one uncle who lived in California, I had no family whatsoever before I gave birth to Miriam. I wasn't keen on losing David's family, too. I happily remained in contact with his father for years.

Some people make the mistake of losing half their family when they get divorced. This can also happen when a spouse dies. Going your separate ways may be unavoidable after a bitter divorce, but many marriages don't end dramatically. All it takes is some effort on your part and you will likely be able to keep those in-law relationships going. And certainly if your spouse has died, it might be possible to reach out to your in-laws to stay involved in their lives. Don't cast aside a pool of companions who already know you and loved you.

How might you do this? On birthdays, make a phone call. Chat for a while. If possible, make a date to see your former mother-in-law or father-in-law in person. If everyone in that extended family exchanges holiday presents, keep up the tradition. Any demonstration of goodwill will help maintain or rebuild these crucial relationships.

Stay Connected to Loved Ones

The oldest object I own is a washcloth. Besides a few photographs of my parents and grandparents, it's the only possession I have from my childhood. Even though there's a pocket for my hand and it would be quite useful when I take a shower or bath, I never get it wet. It's more of a museum piece. I keep it inside a sealed plastic storage bag so I can look at it but don't have to worry about getting it dirty or stained.

I took the washcloth with me the day I left Germany and boarded that train to Switzerland. I packed it in my bag when I left Switzerland for Israel, and I made sure it was in my suitcase when I left Israel for France and later the United States. I am ninety-six years old and I left Frankfurt when I was ten. And while a few of the white and navy-blue threads are pulled and frayed, most of the orange and yellow ones are in good condition, a miracle of sorts to me. I feel objects can convey the relationship you had with loved ones. The washcloth is a reminder of my parents. It helps me feel connected to them.

Family members who are deceased can still be part of your life. Just because they are not physically present doesn't mean their presence can't make you feel less alone. There's a book from the nineties called *Continuing Bonds* that's gained considerable appreciation among therapists for its ideas about connecting with loved ones who've died. The authors argue that our "devotion and affection do not end with a death," and because of that, the bereaved don't need to sever ties with the person they loved; instead, they can continue their relationship through "dreams, memories, conversations about them, and cherished objects that remind us of them."

I also think you can talk to your loved ones.

If your mother died when you were an adult, and assuming you had a good relationship, when you think of a question you wish she were alive to answer, your mind will likely come up with the kind of response she might have offered. You knew her well. Your subconscious is able to paint a vivid picture of what an actual conversation with her might be like right now. And while I wouldn't want you to spend all day talking to your dead mother, if you do it from time to time and these visits help relieve your loneliness, then they're something that you should turn to whenever you need to feel a sense of connection. Don't be alarmed if you get emotional. That's OK and not unusual.

I must tell you one more thing about my washcloth and why it remains so special to me. It's embroidered with my initials, K.S.—for Karola Siegel—in cranberry-red thread. The letters aren't visible from the outside. They're tucked inside the mouth, where your wrist would touch if it were on your hand. The only way to see the stitching is to pick up the washcloth and look inside. And when I do put my hand inside, I'm transported back to Frankfurt and being around my family.

Give Yourself a Break

We all do a good job beating ourselves up. Maybe you've caused your parents, siblings, or children a lot of pain. Shame and guilt may be the reasons you are lonely.

Cut yourself some slack right now.

No matter what you've done, no matter whom you've hurt, don't lock yourself in a fortress of your own making. If you need to make amends, do it. Take steps, no matter how big or small, to repair the damage you've caused. Begin the healing process so you can open yourself up to connections, not close yourself off.

Everyone is worthy of close relationships. Tell anyone in your family who asks that Dr. Ruth says so.

Seek New Family

If for some reason you don't have family, take it from me: You can build a new one. Weaving a family of your own choosing can alleviate loneliness. It doesn't matter why you no longer have family. Maybe, as was the case with me, they've all died. Or perhaps, because of work, they no longer live close by. Does any of this mean you no longer have family to spend time with? Does this mean you have zero support when you need it? My answer is always the same: Absolutely not!

Throughout my life, people who were willing to be close friends, not just acquaintances, were swept up into my definition of family. I could rely on them and they could rely on me. It didn't matter if they lived down the block or on another continent. I put the same energy into maintaining contact with these friends as most people put into staying in touch with their own relatives. I established a new family unit because I longed for that sense of security and unconditional love, the kind you get from family.

What could this look like for you in practice?

Let's say you have friends who live far away. You

haven't been in touch for an extended period of time, so it might feel uncomfortable reaching out. Get over that discomfort! No matter the distance, no matter how long it's been since you've talked, I want you to commit to getting back in touch—and staying in touch.

If your goal is to turn your friendships into family relationships, you have to be proactive. Some friends may be resistant to increasing their involvement in your life, but I imagine most will welcome the opportunity. They'll want to spend more time with you and know you even better. Naturally, to create a family out of your friendships, you need a few good friends in the first place. In the next section, I'll explore exactly how to find them.

Friends and Lovers

Every single person on this great big planet of ours could potentially become a friend or lover. I'm aware this is an overstatement and also probably a little overwhelming, but my goal is to give you hope. Say to yourself over and over again until you believe it: *I am going to make new friends. I am going to find a romantic partner*.

If after repeating these words you're still convinced that you'd need a miracle to change your predicament, know that miracles happen, because to some degree my life has been full of them. But you must never passively wait around for divine intervention or inexplicable good fortune. Friends and lovers generally don't show up one day unannounced. Relationships that matter need to be cultivated.

Finding the just-right friend or romantic partner requires a lot of dating. In many ways, building meaningful connections is a numbers game. You could meet someone and spend a lot of time together, and then, for whatever reason, the relationship fizzles. I suggest bettering your odds by planting many seeds and seeing which ones blossom. Every idea in this "Friends and Lovers" chapter will help.

I've been saying throughout this book that the solution to loneliness is in your hands. Curing loneliness won't happen immediately; it is a deliberate, step-by-step process. Like a farmer, you have to put work into that connections field of yours if you expect it to yield any produce. Coming to terms with this notion will make finding your way less burdensome. It's only if you lock yourself away and do nothing that you're bound to continue feeling disconnected and alone.

The strategies below will guide you in nurturing the kinds of friendships you are seeking—ones that bring you comfort and fulfillment and, when it comes to romance, lots of great sex. And don't discount a miracle or two happening along the way! As long as you're moving in the right direction, there's no telling what might happen.

Broaden Your Friendcabulary

The word *friend* has many meanings. There are casual friends, work friends, friends of friends, best friends forever, childhood friends, fair-weather friends, and friends with benefits. Don't get caught up in the idea that if you don't have a single best friend, you're doomed. I am a strong believer that there are many types of worthwhile friendships, and developing all kinds will make you feel less isolated.

In my life, I've had many types of friends, and each offers me something special. There's my oldest friend and first boyfriend, Putz (pronounced Pootz, unlike the Yiddish insult). We haven't been a thing in decades, and he lives in Israel, but I still feel a deep and satisfying connection to him every time we talk, and he still calls me Karola. And then there's Cliff, whom I met almost forty years ago at the height of Dr. Ruth mania. He had just graduated from college, and I needed help managing my office, in particular the thousands of fan letters I received every week. We formed such a close bond that I brought him along as a personal assistant, then a production assistant, when I launched my nationally syndicated *Ask Dr. Ruth* TV show. Fast-forward four decades, and he usually visits me once a week, at other times we talk on the phone, and because he's in a band, I've gone to see him perform many times.

Another terrific friend is Erik. He's a relatively new friend. Erik lives in my apartment building and we're able to see each other nearly every day, often twice a day. We're collaborating on a musical project that will help bring grandparents and grandchildren together. (You can learn more about the concert we're creating in the September section of "Your Monthly Calendar.")

You might notice that all the ones I mentioned are men. I certainly have many good friends who are women, but I wanted to make a point. You can be friends with anyone, male or female, straight or gay. Don't cut off anyone because you have the idea that a friend must have the same anatomy or sexual orientation as you.

It might be wonderful to have a BFF, but having one is not necessary for living a full and connected life. Don't get hung up on the idea that you need to find a best buddy right away. Right now, I just want you to seek individuals to spend time with and then take your time building rewarding connections with those who seem the most promising.

Curate Your Social Circle

You must be the boss of your social life. When you're decisive about whom you spend time with, when you exercise agency in your relationships, you're better able to nurture the kinds of connections that are built on shared values and interests and bring you joy. If you're keeping people around out of laziness, habit, or inertia—and not because they're genuinely interested in you or make you feel good about yourself—you need to take stock of your connections and make some changes. Your well-being depends on it.

Everyone who knows me well knows that I hate complaining. People who spend too much time grumbling are less capable of offering you positive relationships. My advice is to surround yourself with people who are fully invested in living. Avoid people who whine all the time. They won't lift you up, and they certainly won't expand your world in the way you're hoping for.

This is not an all-or-nothing proposition. There's no need to cut people out of your life entirely, especially if they offer you even a small measure of happiness. Instead, take small steps to grow your circle with purpose. Then, gradually, begin spending more time with these more positive and optimistic people.

Don't Judge a Book by Its Cover

There's no doubt you'll meet someone someday who doesn't seem, at least at first, like a good friend or long-term partner candidate. Try not to judge a book by its cover. If you make a rash decision, you might be cutting yourself off from a connection before it has the chance to start.

I came very close to losing a major opportunity because I was too quick to dismiss it. I was traveling overseas—I don't remember exactly where I was—when Pierre called to say that the publisher of the Dummies books wanted me to write *Sex for Dummies*. I wasn't familiar with the series, so I said, "Tell them no. I don't write books for dummies." But Pierre didn't listen to me. He informed the publisher that he couldn't reach me. He knew I was making a big mistake. When I returned to New York, Pierre convinced me to go to a bookstore and look at some Dummies books. After seeing them, I changed my mind. *Sex for Dummies* sold hundreds of thousands of copies and was translated into seventeen languages.

I admit that when I heard *dummies,* I reacted only to that one word. I was wrong. In your case, don't let snap judgments ruin your chances of developing a good and satisfying relationship. You can build deep connections with people who have different political views and religious beliefs. I bet someone you didn't initially think was attractive may actually grow on you!

First impressions might tell you everything you need to know, but not always. Push yourself to give people a second or third chance. If you do, you might discover someone worth befriending.

Organize Concrete Plans

If you're longing to get out of your house to be with another person, don't be satisfied with superficial, nonspecific phone calls and texts. Checking in to say hello or find out the latest news is an important way to stay active in each other's lives, but you know what's missing from that kind of back-and-forth? Making an actual date to see each other!

The next time you text or call a friend, be the one who suggests a date, time, and place to get together in person. It's better to be proactive than passive. By taking control of the situation, you're more likely to get what you want—a potential partner to have dinner with or a friend who will join you for a walk around the block.

And if they say, "Great idea! I'll get back to you," and then they don't, make certain you call or text them back. Be a little pushy. They might not need to socialize as much as you do, which is why you're the one who needs to do the suggesting. You know what I do? When I say goodbye to a dear friend, I always ask, "When will I see you again?" The question delays our departure by a few minutes, but nobody cares. We get out our calendars (I still use a paper one!) and happily mark another date to see each other.

Set Aside Time

Creating meaningful connections requires work. If it were easy, I doubt the U.S. surgeon general would have felt the urgency to declare loneliness an epidemic. As I said in "Self," you must evaluate your routine and make it a priority. But it will take time.

One pioneering study by Dr. Jeffrey Hall, director of the Relationships and Technology Lab at the University of Kansas, shows that it takes about twelve thousand minutes to develop a new best friend. He also found that it takes at least 120 hours over the first three weeks to develop a good friendship, and more than 200 hours over six weeks to turn a friend into a best friend.

I don't bring this study up, though, to obsess about how many minutes it takes to make a friend. You already know it takes substantial effort. The point I want you to focus on, in addition to the amount of time you're devoting to your social life, is what else Dr. Hall discovered: He determined that it matters what you *do* during that time. You could be in the same book club for years, seeing the same people over and over again, but if you do nothing to advance those relationships, those individuals will remain acquaintances and nothing more. So what to do? For starters, I hope you're already trying out some of the strategies in this book, like being approachable and actively listening. But to supercharge your connections, you must also pay attention to context.

Pay Attention to Context

The spark that drives all kinds of relationships forward is doing activities together. The reason for this is not complicated. Making the choice to have fun together—or deciding to carve out a few moments to have a private discussion—communicates interest, not obligation, and the communication of mutual interest is essential for turning acquaintances into deeper connections.

A friend of mine has a box for the opening night of

the U.S. Open tennis matches. I used to be a regular guest, and so was President Bill Clinton. We'd sit aside from the others and talk and talk, but not about the points or players. Sure, getting those free tickets put us in the same place at the same time, but our physical proximity is not the reason our long-time friendship grew. It grew because we made the choice to break away from the group and concentrate on each other.

Sharing experiences creates opportunities to appreciate people and see them in a new light. It also creates time to nurture relationships.

Talk Openly

You might get to know someone incrementally by joking around, but to strengthen relationships, you must share updates about your life and have meaningful discussions. The best conversations might make you feel uncomfortable, especially at first, but don't give up. (Remember the first time you had sex? Losing your virginity might not have been the best experience, but I am hoping you've had lots of great sex and orgasms since.) Talking openly might feel a bit similar. Just follow my advice. As with good sex, you'll get better at it!

Straight talk helps connections progress. If you disclose that you've lost your job or been recently diagnosed with an illness, the other person will likely feel more comfortable revealing something personal, too. You might even learn that you share a challenge or concern—a struggle that you can talk about more. Exchanging confidences without fear of judgment is how friendships deepen.

There's no doubt that the reason I became so popular on the radio is because my listeners knew they could be open with me. When I'd greet callers with "You're on the air," they knew they could tell me anything and I'd never laugh, snicker, or put them down. Openness is what made my fans and me feel so close.

But please don't take this to mean that small talk is bad. Bantering about your day is the gateway to more in-depth conversations. So when you're comfortable going a little deeper, do it.

Hang Out

Part of what relationships need to become deeper and more meaningful is quality time. What I mean by this is unstructured time, the freedom to sit and talk without anywhere else to go and with nothing else to do. This also means having conversations with no set agenda or goal.

Sheila Liming, author of *Hanging Out: The Radical Power of Killing Time,* has described hanging out this way: "Daring to do not much and daring to do it in the company of other people."

Daring? It *is* daring! And it's hard to believe that hanging out takes thought and work. But it does. I refined my ability to hang out in Parisian cafés. The French make a point of practicing the art of conversation over coffee. As students at the Sorbonne, we were so poor that we'd go to a café and two of us would sip one espresso. We'd sit there for hours commenting on the passersby and talking about writers, painters, ideas. It was an incredible time.

When I was older and in New York, one of my favorite places to spend time was Elaine's, a restaurant on Manhattan's Upper East Side that was often visited by celebrities. I had a friend, Josh, who had a reserved table, and I'd join him every so often. I'd lose track of time just talking and getting to know people. Some people I'd see again, and those people I got to know even better. You never knew who might stop by the table, and that was part of the fun. The conversations were fabulous and freewheeling.

But I think it's important to keep in mind what I never talk about. I don't like gossip. I don't like venting about errands and chores that have to get done—that's so boring! And you already know how much I dislike complaining.

Is there a restaurant or coffee shop near you where you could just hang out? Maybe start small. Invite one friend, and that friend invites a friend, and see how your table grows!

Grease the Wheels

Speaking of restaurants, restaurant owners can teach us a thing or two about creating enduring relationships. Whenever I went to Spago in Beverly Hills, one of Wolfgang Puck's fabulous restaurants, I would get a free smoked salmon hors d'oeuvre. It's not the only reason that I and so many other celebrities would go to Spago, but it helped. And later, after the meal was complete, Wolfgang always came over to my table. We'd speak in German for a little bit, and I loved it.

Should you try to buy your way into friendship? If need be, I say yes. Let me explain.

If several of your co-workers are going out after work, and normally everybody buys their own drinks, you'll score some points with the group by picking up the first round. Is it a bribe? I don't think so. I just think it will help you curry favor and be thought of more positively, like what Wolfgang Puck does so well at Spago. His overture was kind but calculated. It made me like him even more, so that I kept going back to his restaurant whenever I could.

A modified version of this approach can work for you, too. I'm not suggesting you spend so much money that you can't afford to pay the rent, but for the price of a few glasses of wine, you might ease the path to building new and worthwhile relationships.

Throw Parties

When your birthday is approaching, if nobody has offered to make plans, it might be tempting to spend the day by yourself and pout. But you have to take action. Tell everyone you know that your birthday is coming up. Throw yourself a party if necessary. If all else fails, go to a neighborhood bar and announce, "Today's my birthday. This round's on me!" I guarantee people will celebrate with you. And you know what else will happen? The next time you go back to that bar, people will remember and welcome you.

Of course, your birthday only comes around once a year, which leaves a lot of other party-planning possibilities. Invite people to celebrate even the silliest of holidays with you. In the month of May, there's Eat What You Want Day and Chocolate Chip Day. In June, there's Iced Tea Day, and my favorite, Onion Rings Day. (If you want to know why this is closest to my heart, just google "Dr. Ruth" and "onion rings"!)

People might think it a little strange to get together for such harebrained reasons, but then again, if the party sounds fun, they're likely to come. And since deepening your connections is the goal, I say it's smart to be a little creative with how you go about doing it.

Work at Compromise

If you spend a lot of time by yourself, you have something in common with big shots and celebrities: You often get what you want when you want it.

This similarity could be one of the reasons why you're lonely.

What's for dinner? It's up to you. Should you watch TV or read a book? You decide. And on and on. After a while, you become used to a life without friction. You may hardly have to compromise at all.

But compromise builds relationships. When two people don't share the same opinion, there's a period of negotiation that takes place. There's a give-and-take. If you don't have experience compromising, you might become pigheaded. You might become sullen or angry when you don't get your way. None of this is going to help you build and maintain connections.

Every relationship requires compromise if it's going to last. The next time you have a disagreement with a friend or family member, I want you to review it carefully. Were you being too aggressive? Were you looking only to have things your way? I am not saying you should constantly put your needs and wants last. Not at all. But I do want you to decide which battles are important and which ones to let slide. My goal for you is to become adept at the fine art of compromise so you're best positioned to build and enhance your relationships.

Stick with Honesty

When Fred and I were dating, I deceived him. I still consider myself lucky that my little plot didn't end our relationship. I had invited Fred to a homemade dinner. My goal was to impress him, but because I am a terrible cook, I conspired with a distant relative to prepare the meal and pass it off as my own handiwork. Forever afterward, as he was forced to eat all the awful meals I created, he'd bring up the incident when I hoodwinked him into believing that I had made him dinner from scratch.

I realize that this is not the biggest lie in the world, and perhaps you were hoping for something more scandalous, but my sneakiness upset Fred so much that he never stopped bringing it up. I wasn't yet a Westheimer, but it was the Westheimer Maneuver he never forgave. I never should have done it. I was stupid, and the risk was too large. He could have ended our relationship because I had undermined his trust. I got off easy, and I hope you learn from my mistake.

Even lying by omission is a problem. I've always been scrupulous about saying that while I'm entitled to put *Dr.* in front of my name, I'm not a medical doctor. My doctorate is in education. And while I am a seasoned therapist, I never wanted anyone to think that I was providing MD-type advice. If you make yourself out to be something you're not, you're going to be found out. And there's a decent chance that the discovery will end the relationship. It's just not worth it.

Solid connections are built on honesty and transparency. When you're beginning relationships, if you feel the need to pretend that you're richer or more important than you really are, then the people you're hoping to impress aren't the friends and lovers you ought to be with.

Every time you're together, your ego is going to suffer because you'll know that they'd think less of you if they knew the truth. So while I wouldn't tell you to paint the bleakest picture of yourself when meeting someone new, it's easy enough to skirt subjects or activities that will make you look less than fabulous.

Always tell the truth, but maybe not everything all at once. Reflecting on that evening with Fred, after we ate, I could have mentioned to him that I had gotten help with dinner and that he was worth the extra effort. That would have been the better choice. It might have avoided the next thirty-plus years of his near-constant ribbing if I had been honest a lot sooner!

Tell White Lies, Sometimes

In 1947, after living on one kibbutz (south of Tel Aviv) and spending another year on a different kibbutz (next to Haifa), I moved to Jerusalem. I was thrilled to be there but soon got very lonely. I felt like a speck. I remember walking around on Friday nights by myself and looking into the windows of all the houses lit with Shabbat candles. *They all have families. They all have somebody to be with. Why can't I?*

But some aspects of my Jerusalem experience were wonderful. It's where I enrolled in a seminary to become a kindergarten teacher and made many new friends. Yet as my adult life was beginning to take shape, the political situation was growing increasingly tense. On November 29, 1947, the United Nations adopted a plan that paved the way for the British to leave Palestine and divide the land into two states—Jewish and Arab. Because there was so much unrest in the wake of this massive change, Jewish civilians were encouraged to join the Haganah, the precursor to today's Israel Defense Forces (IDF), so that's what I did. (I know you're wondering what any of this has to do with telling white lies and loneliness. Be patient with me. The reason for this story is coming.)

After basic training, I was given many jobs, including messenger and sniper (I still remember how to break down a rifle). I was never injured until the following year, when Israel declared itself a state. Then, on June 4, 1948, my twentieth birthday, I was caught up in a bomb blast. Three people were killed, one of whom was standing right next to me. I felt an excruciating pain in both my legs. Blood covered my feet. The top of one foot had been blown off and pieces of shrapnel were stuck all over my body, including my neck. I underwent surgery and have always felt grateful that I didn't lose either foot. (OK, here comes the point of my story.)

My recuperation was long, and while I was getting better, I became infatuated with one of the nurses taking care of me—a strong man, handsome and blond. Maybe because I had been without my family since I was a little girl, perhaps because I felt so isolated living in Jerusalem as a young woman, I craved his affection and attention. In order to get him to spend as much time with me as possible, I pretended that I needed a little more help than I did. This was my white lie. I lied so I'd feel less lonely. After I was released from the hospital, the nurse and I became romantically involved, at least for a time.

To me, the white lie I told was acceptable. A few extra minutes with me wasn't keeping him from providing critical care to other patients. There were triage nurses for the most serious cases, I knew. How do you tell whether a lie is white, meaning unharmful? It's pretty simple. Consider the day the lie is discovered. Will people think less of you? Might they never want to see you again? Or will they grin and leave your relationship intact?

I am not suggesting that you go around spewing white lie after white lie to win over possible friends and lovers. But if someone suggests you go to the movies to see a romantic comedy, and you detest these kinds of films, saying you like them just demonstrates your ability to compromise. Like my white lie, yours is victimless, and it's unlikely to come back to bite you.

Forgo One-Night Stands

I have long campaigned against having sex on the first date. This is even more important advice if you're lonely.

Some people use the dating scene looking only for physical contact. Once they get what they want, they move on. Casual sex may feel very good in the moment, but afterward, you might feel even lonelier than before.

Sex is emotional. When you're intimate, it's common to envision a future with the other person. But if it turns out that sex was the only thing that brought your partner to the bedroom, you're going to feel worse because your hopes of a more significant relationship have been dashed. You're better off avoiding such situations in the first place and making it a point not to have sex too quickly.

And while love at first sight does exist, more often than not, people need time to assess each other. Someone could seem very nice at first but have a hidden and horrible temper. It's always better to wait and gather more information. Assuming the relationship builds, there'll be plenty of time to have great sex. Until then, I want you to take your time and protect your heart.

Continue Having Sex!

Sex is the glue of romantic relationships. It makes us feel close to our partner. And while some older couples who no longer have sex maintain good relationships, others don't. Without this glue, they become estranged. Each person, no matter how attached and in love they once were, becomes progressively lonelier.

Feelings of disconnection caused by a lack of intimacy are avoidable. For a time, I was actively involved in a clinic at Bellevue Hospital in the Department of Geriatrics to help older adults improve their sex lives. Some men had difficulty obtaining and maintaining an erection (though Viagra came along and certainly helped that group), and quite a few women needed help managing painful vaginal dryness. But with our expert support and information, they could still have sex. Increasing the amount of touching helps. Introducing sex toys such as vibrators and masturbators is useful. And by including the application of a lubricant as part of sex play, couples are able to rediscover great sexual pleasure. What I learned at Bellevue is that you *can* teach older people new tricks, and these new tricks have the ability to reignite passion and rebuild connection.

As you age, it's essential to appreciate the warmth and closeness that having sex brings, even if the intensity of the experience—and the experience itself—is different from when you were younger. Try to make adjustments. See how it goes. If you're still having problems, seek out professional help so that you can stay sexually active as long as possible. Not only will it feel good, but it will also go a long way toward keeping your relationship vibrant and healthy, and you and your partner from feeling needlessly lonely.

Keep the Old

As you've come to know, I am still in touch with Putz, my first boyfriend. He and I met at that children's home in Switzerland, and we became a couple, as much as two kids in an orphanage with very strict rules could become a couple, when I was about twelve.

Having Putz take a liking to me was a wonderful surprise. I had always thought I was too ugly-looking for any boy to want anything to do with me. But he was attracted to me and I was very attracted to him. I remember all the kids were involved in a sewing project one day, and I intentionally placed the piece of fabric I was working on over my upper thighs and lap—not on the table in front of us—so Putz could sneak a quick feel without anyone seeing.

The two of us didn't remain a couple the whole time we were in the orphanage. (I had a tendency to be a little bossy and he soon found someone else.) But we've remained friends all of these years. Even though he settled in Haifa and I made a life for myself in New York, every time I traveled to Israel, which was yearly, we carved out time for a visit. He's one of very few people left on earth who knows what my life was like when I was a child. We have a shared history, which is so important for combating loneliness.

If you can, I urge you to keep old lovers and friends close. I know this is not possible or advisable for everyone. There are very good reasons for cutting people off completely. I am encouraging you to consider the value of keeping old relationships if they were good ones. If the only reason you've severed ties is the passage of time or distance, I'm pushing you to reconsider your decision and get back in touch.

Why should you keep friends and exes in your social sphere? To me, they're like money in a rainy-day savings account. You never know when you're going to find yourself in need of a dear old friend who knew you and cared for you way back when. Yes, make new friends, but keep the old. They become living, breathing pieces of scaffolding that keep you from crumbling when you're feeling especially alone.

Make Yourself More Friendly

What kind of friend or romantic partner are you? Let's assume you're a great listener and you're funny and comfortable sharing your feelings. These are all great qualities. But if you're not generous with your time, none of the other stuff matters.

What happened to Pierre after he lost his wife illustrates my point. Before his wife passed away, he'd turn down many invitations. He was happily married and wasn't looking for additional activities or companionship. But after Joanne died, Pierre came to understand that he no longer had this luxury. He recognized he had to be the kind of person who accepts invitations. Some evenings he might have preferred to stay home with a good book, but more often than not, he was quite pleased that he pushed himself to go out. Being busy helped Pierre feel less lonely.

When I was a young single mother, I could have used my baby daughter as an excuse to stay home. But I decided I wouldn't do that. I chose to say yes to parties and just take Miriam with me, putting her to sleep in any spare bedroom. (It was a different parenting time!) I knew that cutting myself off from people I enjoyed would not be good for either of us. If I had stuck to myself all the time, I would have been doing nothing to alter my sense of isolation, that feeling that falls upon so many single parents.

If you're lonely, you may have to force yourself to be more friendly—to be more social. Nobody will come to your door on a white horse and whisk you away. You've been invited. The going is up to you.

Cast a Wider Net

When my radio show went from being taped to being live, I needed a producer to field listener phone calls. I was assigned a young woman, Susan Brown. Right from the start, Susan and I had to completely trust each other. We'd both be successful if we each did our job well. Not only did we make a great team, but we also liked each other a lot. We chose to have regular lunches together, usually in the NBC cafeteria, and we got even closer. The fact that I was a college professor and Susan had just graduated from college didn't stop us from becoming fast friends. I went to her wedding, and she and I are still friendly today. "You made me feel like an adopted daughter," Susan told me recently. "I wanted your motherly advice on getting married, on my career, and you were always willing to share it."

You must expand your thinking when it comes to the way friendships typically form. From the time we start school, our social circles are most often determined by age—students who are in the same grade as us or perhaps, as we get older, the parents of our child's friends. But why let yourself be put into a friendship box like that?

What's essential for forming new relationships is curiosity. *Don't judge a book by its cover.* Be on the lookout for cross-generational opportunities. They invite the sharing of experiences, wisdom, and perspectives. You don't have to work in radio to cultivate such friendships. You can find them right in your community.

Community

YOU'RE LIKELY ALREADY PART OF SEVERAL COMMUNITIES that will be very helpful in your battle against loneliness. In this section, I'm going to teach you how to take off your blinders. I want you to see the big picture—that meaningful connections are waiting for you in places you've underutilized or completely overlooked.

All around you there are groups of people who come together for specific reasons and purposes. There are work communities (colleagues and professional networks); school communities (alumni associations and student clubs); religious and spiritual communities (churches, mosques, temples, synagogues, and other religious organizations); hobby communities (dancing, cooking, gaming, running); support communities (grief, addiction, caregiving, and other challenges); neighborhood communities (senior centers, libraries, gardening clubs, and civic associations); and, of course, volunteer communities (soup kitchens, food pantries, blood banks, and animal shelters). Have you dabbled with any such groups? Is your participation spotty? *If your goal is to feel a sense of belonging, then you must take steps to belong.*

I appreciate that for many people being active in the community means volunteering to help those in need. But I'm giving you permission to simultaneously focus on *your needs*. When deciding what organizations or activities to join, make sure you consider how they'll help you build relationships. Your goal isn't to connect with as many people as possible. Your job is to investigate and filter. I want you to approach connection making like a treasure hunt. Look for the gems!

Over the years, people who came to me for therapy told me they often felt loneliest at home. Eating dinner in front of the television. Getting under the covers alone, night after night. My advice was always the same—leave.

Go out to dinner. Take a walk. Get outside. Go to the library. Go to the park. Beyond your front door is where all the people are.

Make Your Town Smaller

When I was young, I spent a lot of time living communally, first in the orphanage and later on one kibbutz, then another. It was impossible for anyone to go unnoticed. New York City was a completely different experience for me. I had to work exceptionally hard to introduce myself to neighbors and make meaningful connections. To do both, I made a critical discovery: I had to make New York City *feel* smaller.

I joined organizations. I participated in neighborhood groups. I became a board member of the YM&YWHA of Washington Heights and served as board president for eleven years. During this entire time (now fifty-five years and counting!), I've attended countless meetings and social gatherings and made many good friends as a result. Being part of the Y makes me feel more connected to New York City, like I truly belong here.

Your first order of business is to develop a smaller community within whatever larger communities are easiest for you to access. Have you ever gone to a neighborhood block party? If next week you didn't leave your living room, would anyone wonder where you are? If your answer to either question is "no," you must change your absentee status right now. You must *make your town smaller*.

Be Authentically You

I understand that getting involved in neighborhood organizations may feel like an impossibly large step. If you claim you're too busy, be sure to read the section that starts at the end of page 87. But if what's keeping you away is anxiety, that's a headwind of another sort. The best way to overcome this type of uneasiness is to choose a just-right volunteer opportunity. Don't pick a community activity only because you think it will look good on your résumé or be meaningful to someone else. Pick something that piques your interest. Your enthusiasm for the activity will drown out your nerves.

Sure, I understand that walking into a group of strangers can be terrifying. But consider this: The upside of volunteering is that the people you meet are usually kindhearted and welcoming. Individuals who are grouchy, snooty, or selfish generally have zero interest in giving back.

Be a Mentor

One of the proudest moments of my life was receiving my doctorate in education from Columbia University Teachers College. It's very clear to me why I did well in school. I worked hard, of course, but the other reason was that I was learning a subject I loved, and my degree was the ticket to getting what I most wanted—my first nonkindergarten teaching job.

I landed at Lehman College in the Bronx and quickly learned that being a teacher is one of the best jobs for being socially active and engaged in the community. Bright young people are energetic and will constantly challenge you to think and talk. It's impossible to be around students and not begin to share their joie de vivre, their zest for life. The great news is that you don't have to be a teacher to reap these benefits. You can be a mentor.

Mentoring programs welcome people just because they have valuable experiences to share. If you're an accountant (assuming you're great with numbers!), you can help children with their academics, specifically in math. Maybe you work in human resources and you can prep teens for job interviews and sharpen their cover letters. Or perhaps you could just give your time and listen. Be the person who shows up and really cares.

Like teaching, mentoring is rewarding because you know you're making a difference. You'll feel better about yourself. And mentoring is valuable, too, because it pushes you into new environments. When you're lonely, you don't just need company; you need intellectual stimulation. I've always craved this kind of excitement! In fact, I loved teaching so much that I never wanted to be a full-time sex therapist. I never would have had enough time to teach!

Commit to *Meaningful* Busyness

Too many people boast about being tugged in multiple directions all the time. But there are several reasons why running around frantically is a bad idea. For one, if your attention is diluted, your efforts may not add up to making much of an impact in your community. Second, you'll miss the hidden upside of all of your labor: using your sustained commitment to build richer and more substantive connections.

What does this look like in practice? It's pretty simple, really: If you volunteer every Tuesday night, for example, you will likely run into the same people again and again. A steady and consistent routine can help you build relationships that matter.

In addition to the Y, I've been a member of the committee to protect and manage Fort Tryon Park in northern Manhattan for twenty-five years. Fort Tryon Park is near my apartment, it's where I pushed Miriam and Joel around in a stroller, and it's where I continue to spend many afternoons soaking up the fresh air and sun. The park is important to me, and because of that, volunteering for it feels good. After my husband Fred passed away, the committee named a bench at the park in his honor. I enjoy going there to sit and meditate. If I hadn't volunteered for so many years, if I hadn't invested so much effort into these specific relationships, there's no way that bench would be there today.

Resist the temptation to flutter about town—dropping cookies off here, helping with a tag sale there. Be thoughtful with your time. Try to pick one organization to devote yourself to on a regular basis. Meaningful busyness will always matter more than just being busy.

Help Your Neighbors

The simple act of helping a neighbor can be a powerful antidote to loneliness and isolation. Start by becoming more observant. I don't want you to become a Peeping Tom, but I encourage you to look for ways to be helpful to the people who live closest to you.

If you have neighbors with a new baby, the next time you go to the store, ask if they need food, cleaning supplies, or diapers. Elderly neighbors might need assistance mowing their lawn or shoveling snow off their driveway. I have joyful memories of my mother kneading dough in our kitchen and then sending me off to the neighborhood bakery because we didn't have an oven in our apartment. What a help that baker was to my family! I'm sure you can think of a million ways to be useful. What you do is not as important as offering to do something.

By lending a hand, you'll make new friends. Plus, doing good deeds will definitely lift your spirits. Loneliness can worm a hole in your heart and undermine your self-confidence. It might feel as if you don't make a difference to anyone. If you devote even a little bit of time to helping your neighbors, you'll begin to feel better about yourself and restore your sense of value.

Feign Needs

Just as my family benefited from the generosity of that neighborly baker, I want you to be open to receiving help, too—even if you have to invent a reason to ask for assistance.

If you're too self-reliant, if you're too proud, you're losing opportunities to meet people in your community and possibly forge new relationships. Sure, you can order a container of milk and get it delivered, but how about asking the person next door for a quarter of a cup of milk to finish that cake you're baking? And then you can even drop off a slice as a thank-you.

A word of caution, however: If you're like me and don't really enjoy mixing, stirring, or sautéing (not even when Miriam and Joel were small did I spend any more time in the kitchen than I had to), you might find it more authentic to borrow a hammer or screwdriver. You get the idea!

Those moments when you pick up that extra egg or air mattress are precious. They are pockets of time to deepen connections. And it doesn't matter what you ask for. Just make sure the favor you're requesting is easy to execute.

Reinvest in Faith

I mentioned at the beginning of this chapter that I deliberately joined organizations to make New York City feel smaller. If you haven't looked in a while, you might be surprised by the wide variety of nonreligious events taking place at houses of worship these days. Houses of worship are relationship magnets!

Many activities have little or nothing to do with reciting prayers. Mixers for young adults in their twenties and thirties. Field trips and vacations for learning and exploring. Movie nights and more. Houses of worship are gathering spots. They're social hubs. They're places where you can meet people who live nearby—maybe not in your exact neighborhood, but certainly in the general vicinity.

I do realize we are a society that's been steadily moving away from formal religion for a long time. This is also true of many Western European countries. I also recognize that there's no requirement that you join a house of worship in order to connect with people who share your religious beliefs. (I haven't been heavily involved in any one synagogue in a while, though for a time I did belong to three. If one rabbi asked why he hadn't seen me at Shabbat services, I could always say that I was at one of the other ones!) But because they're social centers, they're definitely worth checking out and potentially adding to your connections-building repertoire.

Read Socially

The great news about being an adult is that you can read as much as you like without being ridiculed for it. *Geek.*

Nerd. Dork. Smarty-pants. While relentless name-calling can be brutal for children who prefer books over people, adults who are passionate about reading can suffer, too—but for different reasons. Reading is usually a solitary activity. We do it at home, in bed or on the couch. But reading can be communal, too, and I want you to turn your love of literature into a means of enlarging and fortifying your social circle.

In your community, or hopefully not too far away, there's a public library. Now, it's true you're supposed to be quiet, but not everywhere, especially if it has social programs that you can sign up for. Yoga classes. Knitting circles. Photography tutorials. Depending on what courses you take, you're likely to encounter neighbors who share your interests.

Independent bookstores have also gotten serious about attracting new customers. Quite a few serve coffee and beer to encourage people to stay for a while—to *hang out*. Some are purpose-built for growing and nurturing communities—readers who love romance books, mysteries, or history, or who identify as Black or LGBTQ.

And there are some very creative folks who have discovered other ways to use books to encourage social connections. In New York City, there's a program called Reading Rhythms. The tagline says it all: "Not a book club. A reading party." The reading parties feature live music and happen in parks and in bars and on rooftops. Even in tattoo parlors! The way it works is that everyone brings a book and reads to themselves, and then blocks of time are set aside for strangers to chat with one another about the book they're reading, first in pairs, then in larger groups.

To me, books are amazing. They can keep you fascinated for hours and hours. But if you're not careful, they can become one of the reasons why you're lonely. They can also cause a massive decorating problem, as they did for me. I once had so many books in my apartment that they could no longer fit on my bookshelves. Instead of getting rid of them, I just piled the overflow in a corner and then covered the stack, which was taller than me, with a blanket. I started joking around and calling the mound my private ski slope. (Eventually interior designer Nate Berkus redesigned a few areas of my apartment for his TV show and the ski slope melted away.)

Sit at the Bar

Bars have traditionally been great places to meet people. But sitting *at* the bar may be your best choice for making connections.

Nobody is made to feel ashamed because they've sat down alone at the bar. Because people sit side by side, at equidistant intervals, it's actually hard to tell who's alone and who's not. Everyone looks the same. You can strike up conversations more easily. And not just with the people who are sitting to your left and right. In front of you, too. The bartender is almost always good for conversation! (If you live by yourself, this is all especially helpful. You may have limited opportunities to talk out loud, to hear your own voice, to chat with another person. At the bar, you can eat a meal and count on conversation.)

Consider how different the social experience is when you're seated by yourself at a restaurant.

When you walk into a restaurant without a reservation, there's no way to avoid the host's or maître d's inevitable question: "How many are in your party?" And then again, once you've been shown to your table, the waiter or waitress will inquire if you're expecting a friend to join you. Within a minute of your answer, the second place setting is whisked away. All of these seemingly innocuous interactions can feel humiliating. You can avoid all of this by heading to the bar.

Bars are also popular spots to go on first dates. While a glass of wine can be good for making those initial encounters a little less tense, I've always cautioned against drinking too much. Too much alcohol can turn any outing into a disaster. (I once put my name on bottles of low-alcohol wine to bring attention to my point. It was called Dr. Ruth's Vin d'Amour. I've never been a big drinker, but it tasted pretty awful. There are much better low-alcohol brands on the market today.)

Admittedly, you may not want to enter a bar because the temptation to drink is too strong. While a variety of nonalcoholic drinks are available, you know your circumstances best, and if going to a bar might be a problem for you, then you shouldn't go. But I think bars are worth exploring. They offer so much more than drinks and food. They offer social activities like dancing, darts, pool, and trivia nights. So if you're able to go to a bar, and you haven't in a while, I suggest giving it a try. You might develop one or two meaningful relationships if you do!

Live in Daily Community

If you feel you've tried everything in your community to build connections and yet still feel like an outsider, you may want to explore a rather bold and alternative living arrangement.

There are approximately six hundred so-called intentional communities in North America, home to more than ten thousand people. No longer derided as "hippie communes," these developments offer residents the opportunity to share expenses, cook meals together, and, of course, build relationships. Many are home to people in their late teens, twenties, and thirties (though many attract people who are much older) and are built with shared interests in mind—living a more sustainable lifestyle or coexisting with more economic equality.

Also created to prioritize connections are specially built neighborhoods such as Culdesac Tempe. The development near Phoenix, Arizona, doesn't allow residents to park private cars, so spaces that would typically be used for parking and garages are instead used for shared firepits, bike and walking paths, restaurants, boutique shops, and courtyards for sitting and talking—amenities that are intended to help residents meet and increase feelings of belonging.

Intentional communities remind me of the kibbutz I lived on when I was a teenager. While I recognize they're certainly not for everyone, they offer a rather different way of living that may be well worth exploring.

You can find collectives in nearly every part of the country and world. The Foundation for Intentional Community maintains a database users can search by location (state or country), type of housing (shared or individual), and organizing principle (faith or social impact). You may also want to explore the Cohousing Association of the United States and the Global Ecovillage Network.

Go to the Office!

I think it's fantastic that there are so many conversations today about where to work—whether at home, in the office, or some combination of both. But for people who are suffering from loneliness, there's no better option than spending time with colleagues in person. I know that it's easier to take care of aging parents or young children when you eliminate the need to commute, but you also eliminate the possibility of running into people in elevators or at the mini kitchen.

The office is where potential friends are. You can have a cup of coffee with a co-worker. You can eat an impromptu lunch together. Back when I was doing my cable TV show, I would tape a few shows during the afternoon and then do another live show in the evening. After the day was finally over at 11:00 P.M., I always had wine and cheese sent to the studio so everyone involved in the production could feel a sense of accomplishment and togetherness. It's nearly impossible to replicate this kind of camaraderie when most or all of your colleagues hardly ever come to the office.

Working in person, while surely less convenient, should be high on your priority list. In fact, I urge you to work only for companies that require workers to come into the office every day or for some portion of the week. None of this fully remote business. My point of view certainly won't win me points with everyone, but that's OK. It may be more convenient to work without leaving your couch, but making the effort to do it in person can really help your social well-being.

Create Remote Connections

Even though I believe that working in person is best for combating loneliness, please know that I am not saying you're facing a lifetime of despair if you work remotely. There are many ways you can strengthen connections with co-workers—even with individuals whom you have little chance of ever meeting in person.

Bestselling author and organizational psychologist Adam Grant writes about the "Five-Minute Favor" in his book *Give and Take*. He says you can deepen your connections by being proactively generous with your time—either introducing people who'd benefit from knowing each other or just sending a heartfelt thank-you email that isn't expected but is sure to be appreciated. The goal is making work relationships, even those that exist solely online, much more personal and satisfying.

While the Five-Minute Favor is effective, it's not Adam's number one recommendation. "My favorite option is to run a Reciprocity Ring—an exercise created by sociologists Wayne and Cheryl Baker," he told me. The way a Reciprocity Ring works, whether participants are in person or not, is that a group of people makes "asks" for something they need or want and the group considers their own "knowledge, resources, and connections to help fulfill the request."

When Adam runs Reciprocity Rings with students at the University of Pennsylvania, where he teaches, he sticks large pieces of blank paper all over the room and invites everyone to anonymously write down their personal or work-related requests. A few of his students were interviewed about the experience and said they enjoyed the exercise because it helped them get to know their classmates on a deeper level. Goals such as "New ways to manage chronic pain" or "Learn how to play the guitar" fueled conversations students might not have had otherwise.

Reciprocity Rings build connections because they make everyone who participates feel good—the "askers" and the "givers." Wayne Baker says the best number of participants to conduct a Reciprocity Ring via Zoom is unlimited, as long as you create breakout groups that are no larger than five to six people.

Cultivate Friends at Work

I've worked outside the home my entire life and met some of my dearest friends because I did. Planned Parenthood, where I was hired as a research associate in 1967, was my first exposure to talking with clients about contraception and abortion. Within one week of taking the position, I knew the job was perfect for me. I loved sex education and talking about family planning. I also enjoyed spending time with so many people! But another benefit of the role was getting to know my boss, Stuart Cattell, and taking our relationship far outside the walls of Planned Parenthood.

You may recall that my late husband Fred and I spent time together at Lake Oscawana, about sixty minutes north of our apartment in New York City. It turned out that Stuart lived close by, and he and I became friends outside of work as a result. The times that I was up at the lake, we hiked together, talked a lot, went sailing, and enjoyed plenty of great meals. Sometimes Fred would join us; other times he did his own thing.

Today I would never advise a subordinate and supervisor to spend time together as Stuart and I did, even if the relationship is platonic, as ours was. Times are different and I don't want anyone to get into trouble. That said, it remains a very good idea to be open-minded about making friends with your peers at work, since work is where you spend so much of your time.

If you work in a large corporate office, employees may be offered opportunities to join affinity groups—maybe ones focused on new parenthood or women's empowerment. Join one of these communities! You might hit it off with a colleague and decide to catch a baseball game one day after work or go to a concert. And remember what I mentioned on pages 66–67 about the importance of paying attention to context? Workplace friends have a better chance of becoming real-life friends when they spend time together outside their shared business environment. Watch out for these kinds of moments. They will help you build rewarding peer relationships.

If you work in an office that doesn't offer formal ways for co-workers to mingle, you'll have to create opportunities on your own. We didn't have formal social programs at Planned Parenthood, either, but we had something else that, looking back now, was a real advantage to feeling connected at work: the absence of computers. To get work done, we had to get up from our desks and talk with colleagues face-to-face.

Throughout your workday, you need to push yourself to stand up from your desk and walk down the hallway. Say hello to colleagues. Ask how their work is going. Offer to help with a difficult assignment. These are all painless actions, yet I promise they will make your work environment a less lonely place.

Cultivate Friends Outside Work

I recognize that making friends at work may not be right for you. If work is the reason you're feeling isolated, build a support network outside of it. Join professional organizations that are designed to bring together people who are at the same stage in their careers, work in the same field, or are grappling with similar issues.

Ann Shoket is the CEO of a community of women and nonbinary leaders called TheLi.st. Just as I suggest in "Be Vulnerable" with regard to relationships with family, Ann says the ability to be honest about career-related challenges helps women feel less lonely at work. She cautions, though, that many women find these types of conversations easier to have when they're with colleagues who don't work for the same company. "We're often in competition at work—vying for resources, attention, and roles that are scarce. These stakes make seeking outside perspectives tremendously valuable and an important way to build a feeling of real togetherness," Ann explains.

Work doesn't have to be a place that makes you miserable and lonely. By joining a professional group, even your local chamber of commerce, you'll create opportunities for sharing your highs and lows. I know being candid isn't easy. But when you allow yourself to be fully seen, you might just expand your number of connections—and deepen them, too.

Go to Conferences

You may work for a business that gives employees the chance to attend professional development conferences. I say, go. Go right now! Don't turn down this very good opportunity for meeting new people because you prefer your home to a hotel. That's an excuse, and excuses hold you back from achieving your goal—forming new and meaningful connections.

And by the way, conferences aren't just for work. There are gatherings for people who are passionate about genealogy, scrapbooking, comic books, gaming, and other pastimes.

I've been a lover of music my entire life, and because of that, I've attended the North American Jewish Choral Festival many times. While the focus every summer is on singing, the festival acts as a typical conference in many ways: Participants hear the latest news from leaders in the field (nearly two dozen accomplished choirs attend from all over the world!), and there are always opportunities to turn strangers into friends.

My friendship with Matthew Lazar, the creator of the festival, became richer over the years because I've gone to these events—so much so that our friendship blossomed well beyond singing. We've shared many meals together and visited Tanglewood, the popular music space in western Massachusetts, numerous times. In 2015, he invited me to conduct a concert at Avery Fisher Hall at Lincoln Center by a group of four hundred student singers. The music made me cry. It reminded me so much of my father, transporting me back to my childhood in Frankfurt. I could almost feel my father holding my hand again as we walked to synagogue on Friday nights. Matty, as we all affectionately call him, made that memorable evening happen for me.

Making friends in a highly curated environment eases the path to friendship. Take advantage of this openness. Use each day to cultivate new connections. You already know you have interests in common, so you've already got plenty to talk about!

Repurpose Community Networks

The reason why Nate Berkus decided I was a good candidate for his TV show is because I'm something of a pack rat. When he came to my apartment in 2011, I was so self-conscious about how overstuffed it was with papers, binders, and tchotchkes that I rarely invited friends over anymore. The clutter was cutting me off from my social life. But Nate put me at ease when he said I didn't have to get rid of everything. He taught me that I just needed to find new ways to manage my cherished belongings. This lesson has a surprising application to this conversation we're having about loneliness.

There's a good chance that you still have access to a few email lists and text chains that were once quite active but are no longer being used. Maybe somebody had a long stay in the hospital and you were in charge of updating friends and relatives about their condition. Or your child was on a soccer team and you had a contact list of parents to arrange carpools. These lists are excellent resources that can easily be put to innovative and deliberate use.

The people on these lists were probably not close friends. You may have enjoyed their company at the time but likely drifted apart because that reason for coming together ran its course. But as I've said, *keep the old*. Friendships are assets to be treasured. Instead of letting these lists go unused, send a brief update that would matter to members of the group. (For example, those soccer parents might love to hear about the new competitive travel team you discovered.) The replies will perk you up, and you might even get an invitation to grab lunch sometime. Deeper friendships will hopefully follow.

If you feel silly reaching out, keep in mind that we're all in this loneliness epidemic together. It's likely that at least one person on those lists is also longing for companionship. To that individual, your out-of-the-blue text or email won't be unwelcome at all; it will be much appreciated.

Join a Support Group

Sometimes, no matter how much of my guidance you follow, the people in your community might not be able to provide the kinds of connections you crave most. You might ultimately need to expand your definition of community to include support groups. There was a time when I needed the help of a psychiatrist, and I sought out a very good one. There's no shame in needing to alleviate a mental health issue any more than in needing to treat the flu.

Unlike the one-on-one therapy I received, support groups offer a concrete sense of belonging to a group. Everyone who signs up is willing to talk and listen and share—a perfect environment to work through individual challenges *and* possibly build connections. If you've gone through a crisis of some sort, like the death of a loved one, it can be beneficial to hear how others are navigating a similar experience. But I do have a big word of warning before you sign up.

A sex therapist like me is considered a behavioral therapist. I went through years of training to do my job. Running a support group well also takes a great deal of study, if you're going to do it with gravitas and expertise. A gathering of people who are permitted to spend an entire session griping about how awful their circumstances are—without being given the necessary tools for making their circumstances better—is not going to be helpful. Worse, it can be damaging.

I know this is controversial. I recognize the value of peer support. But peer support becomes worrisome to me when it's offered in the absence of trained facilitators, especially when participants are given bad advice and group leaders don't have the knowledge to correct it.

So what to do? If you're ready to join a support group, do so, but please make sure it's led by a professional who can move the conversation in a positive direction. When you find that trusted group, it might be the best community you'll ever find.

Technology

YOU MIGHT ASSUME MY ADVICE IN THIS PORTION would simply be to get rid of your technology. But that's not the case. I don't view technology as the enemy. Let me say right away, in case you're thinking that because I'm an older woman I feel otherwise, I would never advise anyone to entirely stop using their phone and laptop. These are necessary tools in today's world. In fact, if you abstain completely, you may find yourself the odd person out, and that won't help you make connections, either.

I have more than 100,000 followers on X, so I can't get on my high horse and condemn social media. It allows me to reach people in a way I could not otherwise. But am I *friends* with them? If I were especially lonely, would these individuals, most of whom I'll probably never meet, help me overcome my sense of isolation? I think you know the answers.

Still, I do think there are ways technology can increase our connections to others, especially in-person connections, which will always be the most important. But what if you don't use much technology, or you use none at all? If you're a technophobe, I suggest you determine if a lack of technology is holding you back. There is an entire universe of invisible social activity happening all around you—invitations to food festivals, cultural events, and more—and if you're not joining in, you will be left out. Perhaps you already are.

Experts seem to agree that technology has become a major factor in causing loneliness. I don't disagree. But it's also true that it can add fuel to your social circle. If used with purpose, technology can enhance relationships. It all depends on whether you use these virtual interactions to build deeper in-person connections.

Break into Conversation Clusters

Outgoing people tend to have an easier time building social connections. Being reserved often makes it harder. But even if you're timid, there are always work-arounds. Perhaps I understand more than most the need to improvise. I'm very short and can't reach most of the shelves in my kitchen. But do I give up when I need something? Never. I use a stepladder. So what am I suggesting you do if you're shy? You need a party-ready version of my stepladder, one that is portable and will help you break into conversation clusters. *It CAN be done.*

Your phone is your stepladder. When you're at a party and feeling hesitant to approach a group of people talking, take out your cellphone and sidle up with a plan: Ask them to pose for a photo and tell them that you're taking it for the host. Nobody will refuse. After they're done posing and laughing, a window will open for you to introduce yourself. Voilà! You're suddenly part of the group!

Just knowing you have a "stepladder" in your pocket will make you feel bolder and more courageous. Even if you don't end up using it, your phone will give you a sense of fearlessness—that you're wearing an invisible superhero cape and have the ability to enter any conversation. It's your secret conversation-starting weapon.

Gift Yourself Seven Minutes

There's another way to boost your connections-making power at social gatherings—and this one requires that you leave your phone in your pocket, at least for a little while: Take seven minutes to become fully invested in a conversation before ending it.

The concept is that you must spend seven minutes talking with someone to determine if the conversation is worth continuing and before giving yourself an out by looking at your phone. The advice is not mine, but I pass it along here because the guidance is from one of the country's preeminent experts in digital technology and has the potential to change your life.

In the field of social science, computers, and cellphones, the best of the best is Sherry Turkle, founding director of the MIT Initiative on Technology and Self and author of numerous books, including *Alone Together: Why We Expect More from Technology and Less from Each Other,* a primer on how technology has created a new form of loneliness, and *Reclaiming Conversation: The Power of Talk in a Digital Age*. Sherry is a clinical psychologist, and her book *Reclaiming Conversation* is markedly helpful in so many ways. But the part that strikes me as the most important for the purpose of combating loneliness is her discussion of the so-called seven-minute rule, a strategy for sticking with a conversation that was told to her by a college student she interviewed for that book.

The student said that for her, seven minutes can feel excruciating. I understand what she means. There's no doubt it might seem like an eternity, especially if you believe there's nothing you and the other person have in common. But the lesson is to stick it out. After a mere 420 seconds, you might discover you went to the same camp or have mutual friends—promising kernels for any new relationship. The student admitted that when she has her cellphone with her, she can't abide by her own rule. This reinforced Sherry's concern that phones distract from our quest to build a less lonely life. "Conversation is the most human and humanizing thing we do," Sherry explained to me. As you likely know by now, I also believe this to be true.

Take Notes on Your Phone

Despite its drawbacks, your phone is the perfect device for keeping track of what's important to other people.

Take notes on your phone whenever friends and relatives mention a brand of clothing they like, a singer or band they love, or a restaurant they're dying to try. Instead of being stumped about what to get them for their birthday or the holidays (and turning to an impersonal present like a gift card), you'll be able to consult your list and buy or make something that shows how much you care and how intently you listen.

Gift giving is an opportunity to convey thankfulness and love. By carefully selecting a present, you're demonstrating that the recipient's interests are important to you, and because thoughtfulness builds closeness, your bond will grow stronger. But don't take notes while you're together. Stay in the moment and focus on your conversation. You can jot them down later, once you're home.

Talk More, Text Less

I've recommended strategies for using cellphones to both establish and deepen connections. But if you've paid close attention, you'll notice something quite ironic. So far, my recommendations haven't involved using your cellphone as an actual phone—*to call people*. Many of us prefer to text these days, but I strongly defend using your phone for its old-fashioned purpose. Hearing someone's voice has the power to make you feel less lonely.

The missing ingredient with texts is voice intonation. Words on a screen can communicate only so much. By using an enthusiastic or unenthusiastic tone of voice, you're able to give a completely different meaning to a word such as *yes*. A simple sigh before saying yes tells the other party that you really might not want to agree but feel compelled to. We learn as infants via mimicry that we can make our voices sound happy or sad, angry or tired. Humans have used pitch and tone to express feelings and communicate emotions since prehistoric times. To throw these vocal cues away in the twenty-first century makes no sense at all.

If you're on a crowded bus, I admit that texting is going to be preferable. But if you always text, your relationships will suffer. And while I am very well aware that you can use your phone to leave voice messages, I don't think audio recordings are replacements for phone calls. Sure, a voice memo is better than a text, but to someone as impatient as I am, waiting to receive a return voice message takes far too long.

By the way, there's a side benefit to talking on your phone. You might not think of it as a means to get your ten thousand steps in, but if you use the Dr. Ruth method, trust me, your step count will climb quickly. When I'm on the phone, I move back and forth incessantly. For me, talking on the phone has always been a form of exercise!

Use Emojis

When calling someone isn't possible or even desirable, using emojis in your texts is the next best thing for getting your point across and not being misunderstood. Emojis improve the quality of texts, approaching the positive nature of phone calls—allowing your messages to be conveyed as you intend. And when you communicate better, your relationships stand a better chance of growing even stronger!

The best way for me to explain this concept is to give you an example. If you text a one-word response to a question without including an emoji, you may come off as terse or dismissive. But if you text the same one-word response—but this time with an excited-face emoji—you are more likely to come off as eager and enthusiastic, which will feel very good to the person who is receiving your text.

What all of this comes down to is the importance of nonverbal cues in protecting and enhancing connections. Even the best actors in Hollywood use facial expressions to ensure audiences know exactly what their character is feeling, in addition to reciting their lines. (In this way, emojis are also an effective replacement for eye contact.) There are thousands of emojis—use some of them!

Remain Cool

Let's assume there's someone new in your life. If this new friend or lover has also been lonely for a while, perhaps you can become very close in a short amount of time. But it's more likely that this new connection has friends and family, so he or she is not going to be able to devote the time to completely fill in your social calendar. If you come on too strong, always texting, this person might decide that you're too needy and begin avoiding you instead of spending time with you.

What I suggest you do at the beginning stages of any relationship is show restraint. Don't text too often, and when you do, make your texts very short. I know the inclination is to reach out. It's a way we try to reassure ourselves that we haven't been forgotten. But pay very careful attention to the replies you get. How quickly do they come? Do they demonstrate enthusiasm or apathy? Unless this new person always writes back fairly quickly and seems appreciative of your communications, you are best served by backing off and remaining cool.

If you're very lonely, I understand that finding a friend is like discovering a life preserver; you want to cling to it for dear life. But even though your reaction is understandable, you need to be patient. If you're not, you might soon find yourself without this connection altogether. So no matter what, in the early stages of a relationship, try to relax and limit how frequently you text.

Immerse Yourself in Podcasts

Podcasts are a fantastic means to be entertained and informed, but some offer much more than music, commentary, and interviews. Some hosts build online communities and create experiences to foster connections between listeners. I want you to search for one or two podcasts on subjects that you care most about, and then do a little homework to determine if opportunities exist for fans to discuss episodes on Facebook or gather in person. Once you find them, don't be passive. Participate in conversations and go to events when they're offered.

Podcasting is an incredible innovation. If I were starting my radio program now, it most definitely would be a podcast! They invite discussion of pretty much any topic and make anyone listening feel less alone in their struggles. I do, however, warn about the temptation to listen to podcasts every time you're in a taxi or running errands. To build more connections, you must unplug your ears, at least sometimes.

Imagine this: You're on the checkout line at the grocery store. It's a very long line. The person standing next to you might want to start a conversation, hoping to commiserate, but they see AirPods in your ears. You may not be saying a word, but you're actually communicating plenty. You might as well be saying, *I'm not interested in speaking with you*. So you know what happens? Nothing. An opportunity foiled by technology. And that's my point.

You no doubt know that couples have met waiting for lattes at Starbucks. But for that to happen, your ears have to be available for conversation. So please, don't use your earbuds as a crutch. When you're trying to make new friends or meet a potential romantic partner, it might be best to listen to podcasts at home.

Chat with Your Seatmate

I love picking up new friends on airplanes! I've met all sorts of fabulous people just because we were assigned seats next to each other. On one flight, I met a dress designer who ended up making me two beautiful outfits. On another, I met a woman who was studying for a master's degree in social work. It turned out that she was Mormon, and I asked her to appear on my show so I could interview her about family life in the Mormon community. The next time you're on a long flight, I challenge you to chat with your seatmate. I'm not suggesting that you strike up a conversation about politics or ask anything too personal, but a little schmoozing couldn't hurt.

Banter of any kind might feel forced to you. I understand. But when the time feels right, push yourself to ask an open-ended question that invites chitchat. You might ask if she's heading home or away for work. If she says away for work, then you might ask about the type of work she does. You may discover you have shared professional interests. I was introduced to John Silberman, who became my lawyer and business adviser for a time, because of a recommendation I received on a plane. John and I have now been in each other's lives for more than forty years!

I recognize that breaking the invisible wall between strangers is harder than it used to be. We no longer have to rely on one another when we travel. Updated gate information is texted to our phones, and we can watch endless TV shows and movies to pass the time. (We were once forced to talk to one another when we were bored!) But here's what I say: When you make the decision to turn off your screen, you're better positioning yourself to make new connections.

I've never been a proponent of abstinence when it comes to sex, and I'm not arguing for abstinence when it comes to phones, either. So I am not saying you should turn off your phone when you're traveling. Your job is to find a middle ground between being entertained and being engaged with people around you. Maybe watch one TV show instead of the whole series. Even in friendship, someone has to make the first move. It might as well be you!

Be *Ruthlessly* Selective

Friends take effort, but you don't need to buy them. Yes, you can certainly spend money on birthday gifts and holiday presents (that's very generous of you and certainly helps grease the wheels), but allowing your bank account to become depleted is never a sign of a healthy relationship, one that is built on mutual affection and respect.

I've heard many stories of lonely people being taken advantage of when they get sucked into digital gaming. In some contests, players compete in front of live audiences and vie for virtual gifts. These virtual gifts cost real money, and if you spend enough, you'll likely be showered with praise. I know this attention feels good—you are being seen and it feels like you're being valued—but it's not real. It's meant to keep you glued to the screen, spending more and more money.

But Dr. Ruth, I hear you say, *I've made so many friends this way. If I cut them out of my life, I'll have no friends at all.*

If you were someone who wasn't suffering from loneliness, you might have a point. But you are suffering. And investing so much time with these types of friends isn't what you need. You need to retreat from these activities and find the interest and energy to meet people face-to-face. You must be ruthlessly selective.

Research Interest-Specific Groups

Now that you've decided to be choosier about how to spend your time and with whom, I encourage you to use websites and apps that are purpose-built for creating connections around specific passions and goals.

One that is very popular is Meetup. Meetups can center around nearly any interest or activity, from drinking coffee to practicing a foreign language to going for a walk. You can find pickup basketball games or running partners. Meetups are especially helpful when you move to or visit a new town or city. An instant way to connect with people—people you might really like and who live nearby!

What I find terrific about these platforms (Meetup is not the only one) is that most of the people who organize activities take their roles very seriously. They try hard to make everyone who shows up feel comfortable. They'll greet you and introduce you to others, and within seconds of arriving, you're part of a group.

Meetups are full of people who are open to making new friends. Will anyone else be lonely, seeking to establish a long-term, meaningful relationship? Some might be. Some may not. But I can tell you this: The odds are in your favor that at the very least you'll establish a few new relationships and have a good time.

Use Dating Apps

Dating in your later years (or any time of life, for that matter) can be daunting. After my husband Fred died, I eventually tried to meet someone new. I went on Jdate, the online dating app for Jewish singles. At the time I used it, it was just a website. It's gotten much bigger since then!

While a few profiles interested me (one man was a therapist, another was five foot two—a real plus, at least for me!), I didn't find a match that excited me enough to keep pursuing. I didn't force a relationship just because being with someone was better than being alone. I am—and you are—too good for that.

I realize that when you're older you may feel a sense of urgency to find a partner. You may not give yourself the opportunity to be choosy because time isn't on your side. My advice: Don't jump into a relationship just because your timeline is compressed. Adjust your timetable. Let go of the urge to land an OK mate when you should be patient and wait for someone who's right for you. Bad relationships can make you feel even more lonely than being alone.

And while my Jdate experience didn't go very far, don't let my experience discourage you. I have friends who've been very successful using dating apps (there are so many you can try), in particular friends who are in their sixties and seventies. The common thread among all of them is that they fully embraced their age and took their time.

Write Honest Profiles

The upside of dating when you're older is that you come to the dating scene much more clearheaded than when you were in your twenties. You know what you want because you have lived experience. This type of self-awareness allows you to be direct in how you present yourself online. If you are a young person reading this, let my personal experience and years working as a therapist save you considerable heartache.

I don't enjoy being in the kitchen, so pretending that I enjoy cooking won't help me find the right partner. I'm better off being honest about my love of skiing. Likewise, if you dislike the beach and you come across a profile of someone whose favorite vacation pastime is sunbathing on a chaise, don't even bother with a first date. You will save yourself a lot of time and energy. And while I realize that dating apps make it very easy to date and keep dating, I advise you to be very careful, and not just when it comes to contraception and sexually transmitted diseases.

Serial dating can make you feel lonely, even more lonely than if you didn't date at all. A constant cycle of new relationships prevents meaningful bonds from forming. It may also cause you to feel a sense of emptiness and a lack of self-worth. These are lessons for everyone, no matter if you're twenty-five or seventy-five. You'll increase the likelihood of finding your forever partner on dating apps if you're 100 percent honest about what you like and what you don't. No pretending!

Go Sightseeing

Book a trip with a tour group or go on a guided tour of your own city. In New York you could go on a historical walk of the Lower East Side, complete with pizza and bagels, or a Harlem walking tour with stops that highlight the Harlem Renaissance and the civil rights movement. You can also use apps, including Google Maps and Yelp, to design your own outing. If you're feeling lonely, invite a friend to come along—a great motivator for getting outside! "Sightseeing is one of the most popular ways to share an experience with someone," podcast host and author Gretchen Rubin reminds us in her wonderful book *Life in Five Senses*.

One last recommendation: On your next visit to New York, bring your family to my neighborhood, Washington Heights, for a trip to the Cloisters, a fascinating medieval art museum in Fort Tryon Park. And when you are there, be sure to rest awhile on the bench dedicated to Fred. It's very close by, an easy stroll from the Margaret Corbin Circle entrance. It would mean a lot to me that you visited.

Track Your Time

Yes, we must live with technology, but we must simultaneously be honest with ourselves about how much we're using it. I support keeping your digital life active, but always with purpose and never at the expense of in-person connections.

The simplest way to find out if you're spending too much time online is to monitor yourself and write down the results. I wish I could tell you there's a certain number of hours that researchers agree makes screen time all good and completely harmless. There isn't. And while no exact number exists, I'd be willing to bet that if you're on your phone so much that it's interfering with your ability to sustain friendships and romantic relationships, you'll see a pattern you'll want to improve when you look at your numbers.

To anyone who says that zero is the only number of hours to spend on technology every day, I completely and emphatically disagree. As I've shared, we can harness technology to build connections. But tracking your time is important because it's a form of accountability. Someone is looking over your shoulder. Someone has your best interests at heart. And that someone is you.

Your Monthly Calendar

HOLIDAYS PROVIDE TIMELY OPPORTUNITIES FOR connecting with others. Some days are obvious (the Fourth of July and Thanksgiving), but celebrations such as World Compliment Day and National Friendship Day are wonderfully relationship building, too. Certain holidays can also intensify loneliness (if your mom or dad has died, Mother's Day or Father's Day might feel especially isolating), and for those times, it's particularly helpful to plan ahead.

I've naturally begun with January. Perhaps you're making a New Year's resolution to build more connections. That's wonderful! But what if you're reading this book in June? Should you put off your search for companionship for another six months? Of course not. I'm an impatient person. I want you to jump to the month you're in right now and just get started.

But I also want you to understand that ridding yourself of loneliness isn't going to happen overnight. You must accept that it's going to take time and acknowledge that success will come only from keeping up the work. This is precisely why "Your Monthly Calendar" will be so helpful to you. No matter the month, no matter the season, there is an immediate and actionable opportunity for making connections. And if you happen to like a suggestion in a month that's far away, go for it. Don't waste a single minute.

Look at the next twelve months as a healthy dessert next to the Menu for Connection. Each offers a fresh chance to beat loneliness and live a happier and more meaningful life.

January

There is no better New Year's resolution than deepening your circle of connections. "Today you" must take care of "future you."

But don't feel bad when you stumble. You can begin now, begin again later, and then begin once again after that. When I make resolutions, I know that I am not going to follow them! There's no need to be perfect. *Be less judgmental* of yourself and stay committed to your goal even when you hit setbacks.

Sure, take advantage of this new start, but don't put all your hopes into it. Keep going when you let your best efforts slide. Continue making the kinds of choices that will benefit you throughout the year—and your life.

February

If the thought of Valentine's Day fills you with dread, do what I do: Call a friend who is also alone and plan to do something enjoyable together. Order in dinner. Watch a movie you both love. And if you eventually decide to go out to a restaurant or bar, who knows, you might even meet somebody!

All of this advice aside, it might help to know that I actually don't believe in Valentine's Day. I think it's a commercial invention that you shouldn't worry about. Restaurants charge more money for dinner and flower companies make all kinds of extra profit. And being bombarded with red and pink hearts all over the place can make people who are not in a relationship feel even more lonely.

Regardless, I understand this day might be hard for you, and because of that, let me offer two more opportunities for lightening your mood.

First, plan a party. My friend Judy Licht, a former television reporter and anchor, hosts a very fun women-only Valentine's Day party every year. You don't have to be single. You don't have to be widowed or divorced. The gathering is just a fun opportunity for friends to express their love to one another.

And last, consider babysitting for a single parent or

a couple with children. You'll not only feel good about yourself because you're lending a hand, but you'll also be so distracted you may even forget for a moment that you don't have a romantic partner—at least right now.

March

March 1 is World Compliment Day. Giving compliments is yet another secret weapon in combating loneliness, just like using your phone to take pictures at parties.

Telling people you like their shirt or mentioning that you like their haircut makes them feel good about themselves, and their positive mood will be aimed in your direction. (Studies show that we often underestimate how good compliments make others feel.) Just pick something you see—a hat, a sweater—and offer a few kind words about it. It's nonthreatening, it's simple, and it works. Plus, it's free!

But compliments don't have to be obvious. The one compliment I most like to receive is that my work as a therapist is taken seriously despite the fact that I am so short. Many times I feared that my work would be dismissed because of my size. If you see me, that's what I'd most like to hear.

April

April 22 is Earth Day. And while there is no shortage of community activities to grab your attention (trail cleanups, nature scavenger hunts), I'd like you to consider spending the day, or at least a portion of it, completely alone. This advice may sound absurd. *But Dr. Ruth, why are you telling me to spend even more time by myself? This is a book about combating loneliness!*

Yes, I know. And no, I haven't lost my mind. The truth of the matter is that virtually any kind of green open space can make you feel less lonely. This is because nature offers alternative ways to connect with the world around us. Being outside—hearing the wind rustling leaves, watching a stream tumbling over rocks—increases our overall sense of well-being. I've always loved being in nature. Focusing on the clouds and squirrels—all of it helps me forget my troubles, at least for a while.

If you're looking for a special spot to commune with the great outdoors, there's one garden in New York City that I like most of all. Friends of my daughter own a nursery in the Netherlands, and when they developed a new kind of tulip, they named it after me. (It is short and has vibrant colors!) Hundreds of these cheerful flowers were planted not too far from my apartment in my beloved Fort Tryon Park. They named the garden Dr. Ruth's Tulips. Maybe on Earth Day you can visit my tulips.

May

If you're grieving the loss of your mother, Mother's Day can make you feel especially lonely. My mother's name was Irma Hanauer, and I remember what she said to me when she put me on that train in Germany to save me from the Nazis: "Be good. Study hard. It will be nice in Switzerland. And we will see each other again."

Her words gave me hope and sustained me through many dark times. Looking back now as I approach my hundredth birthday, what I mostly feel is awe. Her courage astounds me. I can't imagine feeling so afraid for my daughter's life that the best option was putting her on a train to a place I'd never been, to a land and people I didn't know.

When I remember my mother, though, I don't dwell on any of this. I focus on the wonderful ten years we had together. Given my experiences with loss (both personally and working with so many clients over the years), I have three pieces of advice if you're feeling lonely on Mother's Day.

First, be grateful. If you had a positive relationship with your mother, rejoice in that knowledge. (Many clients I treated in private practice did not have good relationships with their mothers, so this shouldn't be taken for granted.)

Second, set aside time to think about your mother, even if there's been a rift in your relationship or you've never been emotionally close. Loneliness burrows deeper when you ignore your emotions and pretend you're OK when you're not.

And finally, if you don't begin to feel better and a

little more connected to your mother, pick up the phone and call a friend. But don't reach out to someone who will cut you off after a few minutes because they're too busy. Choose a person who will let you talk and talk. I predict you will gradually feel less alone if you take my advice.

June

For many people, food increases sensations of connection and love. If you're missing your dad on Father's Day, no matter the reason—maybe you're estranged or he's passed away—you can use your senses of taste and smell to feel closer to him, and in doing so, I hope you will feel a little less lonely.

My father, Julius Siegel, often made me a special meal when I was growing up. Concerned about my growth, he prepared runny soft-boiled eggs and cut bread into long strips for dipping. It was meant to spur my appetite, which was often nonexistent when I was young. (Now I eat plenty. Especially chocolate!) When I think back, I also remember my father buying me vanilla ice cream every Friday night on the way to synagogue before the sun went down.

Are there dishes or desserts that remind you of your father? By eating these foods, by savoring them, you might begin to rebuild your connection and feel it even more strongly.

July

During my journey to America on the French ship *Liberté,* I was in fourth class, and those of us housed way down below weren't allowed up on the top deck. But the night we were due to arrive in New York Harbor, Dan (the man who became my second husband) and I sneaked up top and waited all night, hidden in the dark, to catch sight of the Statue of Liberty. There was no way I was going to miss the view the next morning. I was overjoyed to be coming to the United States and was so thankful to the U.S. Army for defeating the Nazis. I wanted so badly to see the country where these brave GIs had come from to rescue us!

People in the United States often forget how lucky they are to live in a free society. You may be lonely, but it's within your power to change your circumstances. You don't have to be afraid that your neighbors might tell the secret police if you associate with the "wrong sort" of people or that your co-workers will report you for mingling with the wrong crowd. For the most part, while outside forces certainly contribute to feelings of loneliness, we all have the freedom to make positive changes in our lives, to make ourselves happier. This autonomy is one reason I like to celebrate Independence Day. The holiday is also a great excuse to nurture connections in your community!

Join a Fourth of July committee. Plan the local parade or help keep the fireworks display safe. Since organizing these types of events usually takes a while, you'll be planning with the same group of people, and that consistency will strengthen your ties to neighbors. On a smaller scale, if you know that the mom or dad next door is serving in the military, you might include his or her spouse and children in your barbecue plans. I know I always like to be invited places. It makes me feel good that people want to be with me. You can make your neighbor feel good and included, too.

August

National Friendship Day is the first Sunday in August. The holiday is an outstanding reminder to express gratitude for the friends you have. I absolutely treasure my friends because they replaced the family I lost. I thank them for every phone call, for every letter, for every visit to my apartment. Every one of my friends knows how much I care for them, because I tell them.

We risk losing friends when we take them for granted. As you'll read in my conversation with U.S. Surgeon General Dr. Vivek Murthy, he once became so consumed with work that he didn't make time for his most important relationships. "I felt ashamed to reach out to friends I had ignored," he wrote in *The New York Times*. National Friendship Day comes in handy because it's a gentle reminder to let your friends know how much you care about them.

Here's what I suggest you do on National Friendship Day: Write down a short list of friends. Send each one a text or an email. Better yet, pick up the phone. No matter how you reach out, the goal is the same: Tell your friends that you cherish them. Not only will they feel joy, but you will feel a surge of joy, too. (Expressions of gratitude have been proven to increase happiness.) A win-win proposition!

Gratitude has the power to deepen relationships and make them more meaningful. By telling your friends you're thankful for them, you're affirming their value. And who doesn't want to hear they're appreciated?

September

I received so much love from my grandparents during my childhood that when I became a grandmother, I was a superdoter! (One of my most treasured memories is the time I took my grandson Ari to an arcade and surprised him at one of those target-shooting games. Remember, I was a sniper. We came home with an armful of stuffed animals. He couldn't believe it!) The relationship between grandparents and grandchildren is so special to me that I've written several books about it and I'm now developing a concert, "Ruth Grandmother to the World," with my conductor friend Erik, the neighbor I told you about in "Friends and Lovers." And it's why I want to focus your attention on National Grandparents Day.

National Grandparents Day is held the first Sunday after Labor Day, and it's the perfect excuse for grandchildren and grandparents to spend time together. Since grandparents are usually the ones to give to their grandchildren, on this day, grandchildren can reverse roles and do fun or useful things for their grandparents—bake them a pie, watch a ball game together, help make their sluggish computer run faster. When grandchildren set aside time for their grandparents, their special bond has the chance to grow.

I'm very much aware, however, that not every grandparent gets to have these kinds of quality moments with their grandchildren. And this is why I also want to focus on the possibility of becoming a surrogate grandparent, if only for the day. Talk with your neighbor in advance. Offer to take her son or daughter for ice cream on National Grandparents Day. Ask the kinds of questions that grandparents often do—such as how they're doing in school and who their friends are.

There are formal ways to get involved, too. Many websites and Facebook groups are devoted to surrogate grandparenthood. Some even offer matching services. The New York City Department for the Aging, an agency I work with as New York State's Ambassador to Loneliness, has a Foster Grandparent Program that connects individuals who are fifty-five and older with children and young adults to support their academic, social, and emotional development. Not only does this reduce loneliness among older people by keeping them engaged in their communities, but it also helps reduce ageist stereotypes by fostering intergenerational connections. Similar programs are in place nearly everywhere—all you have to do is search for them to participate. When you do, not only will you feel good and have a good time, you'll be building a more connected community, and that helps everybody.

October

We didn't celebrate Halloween back in Germany when I was growing up. It's one of those holidays that hadn't yet made it across the ocean from America, though eventually it did, but long after I'd left. I've since enjoyed lots of Halloween parties. I once dressed up as Charlie Chaplin—complete with a suit, felt hat, and mustache. It was by far the best costume I've ever worn. I even imitated his waddling walk!

If you're feeling lonely, you might want to just turn off the lights on October 31 and pretend you're not home. But in the spirit of deepening your connections with neighbors, I urge you to think again.

Parents of young children tend to accompany their kids when they go trick-or-treating. This presents an ideal opportunity for you to show off what a fun-loving and welcoming neighbor you are!

Don some garish costume. When kids ring your

bell, greet them profusely as you give them candy. If you're dressed as a witch, give a loud cackle. Not only will the children appreciate it, but their parents will, too—and that's the whole point. The parents, not those little princesses and gremlins, are your real audience. My hope is that the next time you see each other, sometime after Halloween, it'll be that much easier to say hello.

November

I've always loved Thanksgiving because it's a major holiday but not a religious one. It binds all of us together and is inclusive of all religions, all denominations, even nonbelievers. But the pressure to come together may make you dread Thanksgiving. You may have nobody to share the day with, or maybe you feel anxious because you have to spend the afternoon and evening with family members who make you feel bad about yourself. I offer a few solutions.

First, adjust your expectations. Thanksgiving hardly ever looks like the idyllic gatherings you see in the movies. So much of the time families bicker, the turkey is dry, and somebody ends up in tears. Most dinners fall way short of what we think they should be like, and this is the reality check I want you to keep in mind.

Second, *be vulnerable,* but this time with your friends and neighbors. If you are not open and honest, not even with one friend, how will anyone realize that you have nowhere to go on Thanksgiving? Don't hide your situation. *Communicate your needs.*

And last, make a plan for next year. Very few problems fix themselves. You must be proactive.

December

The first day of winter is also the longest night of the year. This is why so many holidays in December are associated with light, to counterbalance all that darkness. If there's one lesson I've most wanted to pass along to you in this book, it's that you have the power to make your life bigger—and brighter.

If you are lonely, you likely feel the heavy weight of isolation. The world may feel very bleak sometimes. Listen to me: Do not give in to loneliness. When it is dreariest, when it is coldest and most gloomy, there will be warmth and sunlight again. Follow the advice I've given you, bit by bit. Just hold on for the thaw.

When I was in the orphanage in Switzerland, especially when the letters from my parents stopped coming, there were certainly days when I felt so unbearably lonely that I wanted to give up. My past had been wiped away and my future was very, very uncertain.

But look at me now. Nobody would have predicted—certainly not those who picked on me for being so ugly and short—that I would one day be a world-famous therapist or the first Ambassador to Loneliness of any state in America. Hold up my story as a light until you discover your own.

Life may be bitter for you now, but I am certain it has every chance of getting better. Change won't happen, though, if you hide in darkness. Work hard to cultivate the kinds of connections that bring happiness and meaning into your life. *It CAN be done.*

A Special Conversation with U.S. Surgeon General Dr. Vivek Murthy

Dr. Ruth Westheimer: I've shared a lot in this book about my own battles with loneliness. Readers might be surprised to learn you've also suffered from loneliness. At times in your life, you have lived alone, and you'd sometimes go days without seeing anyone in person. How did you start building meaningful connections?

Dr. Vivek Murthy: I started building meaningful connections by being more intentional in my engagement with others. I was more proactive about reaching out to family and friends, even if it was for five minutes to say I was thinking about them. I also made the time we had together count by giving them my full attention; I wasn't always good at this, but I tried hard. And I made it a point to support or help a friend when they were in need. I realized that helping others was actually good for me—it got me out of my isolated cocoon and helped me feel like I had something valuable to offer the world.

RW: *The Joy of Connections* offers one hundred ideas and opportunities for creating fulfilling relationships. In your view, what is the very first step someone should take to feel less lonely?

VM: Cultivating connection doesn't have to be complicated—you can start by protecting a few minutes each day to reach out to someone you care about. You can express your gratitude to them, offer support, or ask for help. These small steps can make a big difference in how connected you feel and in your overall health and well-being.

RW: Too many people are embarrassed to admit they're feeling disconnected and alone. I'm trying to combat this kind of shame in my work as New York's Ambassador to Loneliness. What are you doing as U.S. surgeon general to address this big taboo?

VM: I've struggled with loneliness throughout my life and have experienced that shame myself. I issued a Surgeon General's Advisory on loneliness and isolation to have a more public conversation about an experience that millions of us have but are reluctant to talk about. I recently completed a college tour where I traveled across the country speaking to young people about the disconnection they're feeling and sharing steps we can take to build a more connected life. In speaking more openly about loneliness, we can help one another understand that we are not alone in feeling alone.

RW: Americans have been growing increasingly lonely over time. What moved you to proclaim loneliness an epidemic in the United States? The problem didn't start with Covid, did it?

VM: Although it was made worse by the Covid pandemic, loneliness and isolation have been widespread challenges for many years. I released a Surgeon General's Advisory because I was concerned about the severity and sheer number of Americans experiencing disconnection in their lives. I wanted people to know how common this was and how consequential it was to our physical and mental health. Being socially disconnected increases our risk of depression and anxiety as well as heart disease, dementia, and premature death.

RW: What's changed since you issued the advisory?

VM: Since it came out, cities, organizations, groups, and schools have been looking seriously at the loneliness crisis and working to improve connection and build community. Counties and states have put together strategies to address loneliness in their communities; members of Congress have worked to design policies to promote social connection; educational institutions are developing programs to help students build healthy relationships; and many faith organizations have shared with me that they are talking more openly about loneliness with their congregations. Loneliness is being recognized as a problem not only in the United States but throughout the globe. Last year, I became the cochair of the WHO Commission on Social Connection to start addressing loneliness on a global scale.

RW: My book is not about the physical health consequences of loneliness, but I realize they are considerable. Can you please outline what concerns you most?

VM: The health consequences of loneliness extend far beyond mental health to include physical health impact. Social disconnection is associated with an increase in mortality that is comparable to smoking daily and even greater than that which we see with obesity. People experiencing prolonged loneliness and social isolation are also at greater risk of diabetes and stroke, in addition to the concerns I previously mentioned.

RW: I've used behavioral therapy to help people overcome difficulties in their sex life. At what point would you advise someone who is very lonely to seek professional support?

VM: Loneliness is a natural feeling we all experience from time to time. It's like hunger or thirst—a signal that something essential to our survival is missing. But when loneliness extends for long periods of time, it can begin to impact our health and well-being. If your feelings of loneliness are persisting despite your best efforts, if they are making it hard for you to function in your day-to-day life, or if they are leading you to consider harming yourself in any way, that would be a sign that you should reach out for help to a trusted professional. You can always call or text 988, the mental health crisis line, at any time to get connected to support.

RW: You've admitted that after serving as surgeon general for the first time in the Obama administration that you felt particularly lonely. You wrote in *The New York Times*:

> I was suddenly disconnected from the colleagues with whom I had spent most of my waking hours. It might not have been so bad had I not made a critical mistake: I had largely neglected my friendships during my tenure, convincing myself that I had to focus on work and I couldn't do both.

So my question is this: Have you appointed your own ambassador to loneliness? (I discuss how important this is on pages 43–44.) Who looks out for you when you are working so hard?

VM: My wife is often the first to recognize when I'm really struggling. I also rely on my friends Sunny and Dave, whom I call regularly to talk about the issues that are most on my mind and heart. Years ago, we decided to form a *moai,* drawing on an Okinawan tradition where a small group of people come together to make an explicit commitment to have one another's backs. My *moai* with Sunny and Dave has literally changed my life.

RW: What gives you hope as we all work together to help people build more connected and meaningful lives?

VM: We all have a fundamental need for human connection. It's the common thread that binds us together. Everywhere I go, I find people are eager to talk about how to build more connection in their lives. I have encountered schools, workplaces, and mayors who are doing the hard work of building programs that will bring people together and nurture healthy relationships. I'm also encouraged by the fact that a little bit of connection goes a long way to helping address loneliness. The most powerful antidotes are often found right around us, in family members, neighbors, work colleagues, friends with whom we've lost touch but who are often just as eager to reconnect as we are.

Further Resources

I hope you have found *The Joy of Connections* helpful. To learn more about loneliness and ways to combat it, visit my co-author Allison Gilbert's website, allisongilbert.com, where she has curated multiple lists of additional resources, including books, articles, and organizations that are researching social isolation and helping individuals build more substantive and joyful connections.

Books

Loneliness has become a popular topic for discussion, and many books address this urgent public health crisis. I reference some of these in *The Joy of Connections,* while others helped me better understand the underpinnings of happiness and the formation of meaningful relationships.

In addition to the books I have mentioned, many others are worth exploring. A select group is noted below.

Brooks, Arthur C., and Oprah Winfrey. *Build the Life You Want: The Art and Science of Getting Happier*. New York: Portfolio, 2023.

Cacioppo, Stephanie. *Wired for Love: A Neuroscientist's Journey Through Romance, Loss, and the Essence of Human Connection*. New York: Flatiron Books, 2022.

Heng, Simone. *Let's Talk About Loneliness: The Search for Connection in a Lonely World*. Carlsbad, CA: Hay House, 2023.

Radtke, Kristen. *Seek You: A Journey Through American Loneliness*. New York: Pantheon, 2021.

Waldinger, Robert, and Marc Schulz. *The Good Life: Lessons from the World's Longest Scientific Study of Happiness*. New York: Simon & Schuster, 2023.

Studies and Reports

Social isolation is the subject of numerous scientific investigations. Researchers are analyzing the causes of disconnection and the profound ripple effects it has on our physical health and mental well-being. Similarly, they're examining the pillars of successful and fulfilling human bonds. I include a small number of these reports and studies here, some of which I have referenced in *The Joy of Connections*.

Boothby, Erica J., and Vanessa K. Bohns. "Why a Simple Act of Kindness Is Not as Simple as It Seems: Underestimating the Positive Impact of Our Compliments on Others." *Personality and Social Psychology Bulletin* 47, no. 5 (2021): 826–40.

Epley, Nicholas, and Juliana Schroeder. "Mistakenly Seeking Solitude." *Journal of Experimental Psychology: General* 143, no. 5 (2014): 1980–99.

Hall, Jeffrey A. "How Many Hours Does It Take to Make a Friend?" *Journal of Social and Personal Relationships* 36, no. 4 (2019): 1278–96.

Murthy, Vivek H. "Our Epidemic of Loneliness and Isolation: The U.S. Surgeon General's Advisory on the Healing Effects of Connection and Community." 2023. surgeongeneral.gov/connection.

TheLi.st in partnership with BSG and Berlin Cameron. "10 Minutes to Togetherness, 2024 Research Report and Tool Kit." Accessed May 12, 2024. 10minutestotogetherness.com.

Organizations

Stay informed and connected with leading experts and organizations dedicated to understanding and addressing loneliness.

Coalition to End Social Isolation and Loneliness
endsocialisolation.org

WHO Commission on Social Connection
who.int/groups/commission-on-social-connection

Foundation for Social Connection
social-connection.org

Global Initiative on Loneliness and Connection
gilc.global

Be in touch on social media

Dr. Ruth's X account is being updated by Pierre Lehu
X: @AskDrRuth

Allison
Instagram, Facebook, X, and LinkedIn: @agilbertwriter
YouTube: @allisongilbert

Monthly updates

Sign up for Allison's free monthly newsletter at allisongilbert.com/subscribe/. There, she will continue the conversation about loneliness and reveal even more strategies for developing and nurturing connections. She will also share updates on her other writing projects. I highly recommend it!

Email us!

We're excited to learn the strategies you're using to beat loneliness and live a happier and more meaningful life. Email Pierre and Allison at connections@allisongilbert.com.

A Timeline of Dr. Ruth K. Westheimer's Life

1928	Karola Ruth Siegel born in Wiesenfeld, Germany
1939	At ten and a half years old, placed on Kindertransport train in Frankfurt to escape the Nazis, began living in orphanage in Heiden, Switzerland
1945	Immigrated to Palestine, changed name to Ruth
1948	Bomb blast caused serious injuries on twentieth birthday
1956	Arrived in New York on the ship *Liberté*
1957	Miriam (Bommer) Westheimer born
1959	Received master's degree in sociology from The New School
1961	Married Fred Westheimer
1963	Joel Westheimer born

1970–1979	Earned EdD from Columbia University Teachers College, studied to be a sex therapist, and opened a private practice
1980	Began radio career with taped show on WYNY-FM titled *Sexually Speaking,* which went live with listener calls the following year
1981–1990	Had radio show go national and became an icon, making frequent appearances on late-night television, writing books (*The Joy of Connections* is her forty-sixth), hosting several cable TV shows, appearing on the cover of *People* magazine, and giving lectures around the world
1997	Fred Westheimer died
2000–2022	Continued giving lectures and making appearances, taught at Yale and Princeton at the same time, published more books; play *Becoming Dr. Ruth* and documentary *Ask Dr. Ruth* produced about her life
2023	Appointed Ambassador to Loneliness by New York governor Kathy Hochul
2024	Published *The Joy of Connections* to address the loneliness epidemic

Acknowledgments

From Dr. Ruth

To the memory of my entire family who perished during the Holocaust. To the memory of my late husband, Fred, who encouraged me in all my endeavors. To my current family: my daughter, Miriam Westheimer, EdD; son-in-law, Joel Einleger, MBA; their children, Ari and Leora, JD, and her husband, Elan Kane; my son, Joel Westheimer, PhD; daughter-in-law, Barbara Leckie, PhD; and their children, Michal and Benjamin. I have the best grandchildren in the entire world!

Thanks to all my many family members and friends for adding so much to my life. I'd need an entire chapter to list them all, but some must be mentioned here: Pierre Lehu and I have now collaborated on two dozen books; he's the best minister of communications I could have asked for! And Allison Gilbert, an excellent reporter and writer, has been a true find as both a collaborator and a friend.

My neighbor who ever since my illness visits me twice a day, Maestro Erik Ochsner, and his partner, Masataka Suemitsu; my longtime friend, fellow board member, and "legal muscle" Jeff Tabak, Esq., and Marilyn Tabak; Cliff Rubin, my assistant (thanks!); my aides, starting with Shkurte Tonaj, who's been with me for more than fifteen years, as well as Tameka McLeod, Marcia Brown, and Arlene Wedderburn; Larry Angelo; Dr. Peter Banks; Peter Berger, MD; Simon and Stefany Bergson; Nate Berkus; David Best, MD; Tom Chapin; Frank Chervenak, MD; Richard Cohen, MD; Martin Englisher; Cynthia Fuchs Epstein, PhD; Nily Falic; Tovah Feldshuh; John Forster; my former neighbors and friends Raul Galoppe and Michael Berra; Meyer Glaser, PhD; David Goslin, PhD; Herman Hochberg; David Hryck, Esq.; Annette Insdorf and Mark Ethan; Steve Kaplan, PhD; Rabbi Barry Dov Katz and Shoshi Katz; Bonnie Kaye; Patti Kenner; President Jack Kliger and the other board members and staff at the Museum of Jewish Heritage, including Haley Coopersmith; Harold Kopliwicz, MD, and Linda Sirow; Robert Krasner, MD; Nathan Kravetz, PhD; Marga Kunreuther; Dean Stephen Lassonde; Matthew and Vivian Lazar; Rabbi and Mrs. William Lebeau; Rosemary Leckie; Hope Jensen Leichter, PhD; Judy Licht; Jeff and Nancy Jane Loewy;

John and Ginger Lollos; Sanford Lopater, PhD, and Susan Lopater; David Marwell; Marga Miller; Jeff Muti; Peter Niculescu; Walter and Debbie Nothmann; Dale Ordes; Frank Osborn; Rabbi James and Elana Ponet; Leslie Rahl; Bob and Yvette Rose; Debra Jo Rupp; Larry and Camille Ruvo; Rose Schreiber; Daniel Schwartz; Amir Shaviv; David Simon, MD; John Silberman, Esq.; Jerry Singerman; Mark St. Germain; Henry and Sherri Stein; Malcolm Thomson; and Maurice Tunick.

A special thanks to New York governor Kathy Hochul; New York state senator Liz Krueger; U.S. Surgeon General Dr. Vivek Murthy; our fabulous agent, Peter Steinberg, and his assistant Harry Sherer; and to all the people at Rodale Books and Penguin Random House who worked so hard to bring this book into the world: Matthew Benjamin, Mia Pulido, Kelly Doyle, Christina Foxley, Keilani Lum, and Cindy Murray.

From Allison

My greatest debt is, not unexpectedly, to Dr. Ruth Westheimer. We met for the first time when I was reporting for *The New York Times* on her becoming New York State's Ambassador to Loneliness. More than a year has passed since that initial meeting, and it's not hyperbole for me to say that she has become—after spending nearly every week since writing this book together—one of my most treasured relationships. I am honored that you entrusted me with this project and absolutely blessed to have been swept up into your expansive definition of family. You make everyone who knows you feel special, including me.

My gratitude also goes to Pierre Lehu, a wonderful collaborator. Your know-how helped coalesce the many critical threads presented here. The process of writing produced more than a groundbreaking book on overcoming loneliness and finding belonging—it created a new friendship, and for that, I am especially thankful. I am fortunate that Kate Buford and Tovah Feldshuh made the all-important introduction.

And while I will save you from repeating many of the names Dr. Ruth has already highlighted, I must double down on just a few. Profound appreciation to Joel Westheimer and Miriam Westheimer (and their families) for their outsize kindness and indefatigable assistance. And to Peter Steinberg, my literary agent at UTA: Your immediate belief in this book and bold advocacy for it were breathtaking. I am lucky to have your support and the backing of such a top-notch team. And to our editor, Matthew Benjamin: Thank you for championing this book with such urgency and care. Your counsel was wise and your thinking was clear. Every page was enhanced because of you.

To all the experts and authors who contributed immeasurably to this book, either directly or by providing resources and guidance, including U.S. Surgeon General Dr. Vivek Murthy, Judy Blume, Adam Grant, Dan Harris, Sunny Hostin, Gretchen Rubin, Wayne Baker, Cheryl Baker, Daniel Greenberg, Jeffrey Hall, Ryan Jenkins, Steven Van Cohen, Gregory Rose, Derek Penslar, Tom Worcester, Rob Maloney, Quill Kukla, Joseph Stramondo, Rabbi David Holtz, Ann Shoket, Sherry Turkle, Richard Weissbourd, and Julianne Holt-Lunstand. I also want to express my deepest gratitude to Traci Doromal, Katie Dealy, Jane Richter, and Rocio Cruz.

Special recognition to Abby Santamaria, Heather Clark, and Laurie Gwen Shapiro—dear friends who were sitting with me at a raucous dinner when the seed for this book began to take hold—and Lisa Belkin, Christina Baker Kline, Laura Mazer, Eve Kahn, Amy Reading, Carla Kaplan, Christine Cipriani, and Sara Catterall, who always lift me up and make me feel seen and valued. I am especially grateful to Bill Ferguson, editor exemplar at *The New York Times*. It's reasonable to assume that without our work together on "Dr. Ruth Saved People's Sex Lives. Now She Wants to Cure Loneliness," this book would not exist. I've been the beneficiary of your craftsmanship and expertise more than once, and for that, I count myself one very fortunate writer.

My dearest friends from elementary school, high school, college, and now—Kristin Brandt, Betsy Cadel, Tracy Costigan, Brooke Edgecombe, Nancy Friedman, Tanya Hunt, Holly Rosen Fink, Rachel Lehmann-

Haupt, Carley Knobloch, Deniz Ayaz Mullis, Jen Ross, and Janet Rossbach. You make my life bigger in all meaningful ways.

And to my family: Mark, my husband and best friend since we met at sleepaway camp, and Jake and Lexi, our smart, kind, and lovable children. You are worthy of the kinds of relationships that make you feel joyful and whole. The three of you are my most prized connections.

From Pierre

Thanks to my immediate family, who have supported me so much since the passing of my beloved wife, Joanne Seminara: my son, Peter Lehu, daughter-in-law, Melissa Sullivan, and my grandsons Jude and Rhys, and my daughter, Gabrielle Frawley, son-in-law, Jim Frawley, granddaughter, Isabelle, and grandson James Joseph; and to those friends and family who have helped me overcome my own feelings of loneliness, including the entire Seminara clan, Peter Zagare, and Gali Neufeld.

A special thanks to everyone who has made this book possible, starting with our agent, Peter Steinberg, whose own connections got us a deal within what seemed like seconds, and his assistant, Harry Sherer. Thanks to all the people at Rodale Books whose efforts helped us bring this book into the world: Matthew Benjamin, Mia Pulido, Kelly Doyle, Christina Foxley,

Keilani Lum, and Cindy Murray. And to my teammate with whom I spent so many hours laboring hand in hand, or should I say mouse in mouse, to formulate, write, and dot every *i* and cross every *t,* Allison Gilbert, thank you, thank you, thank you. Without your discipline, this book would be far less helpful to our readers.

And, of course, a great big thanks to Dr. Ruth Westheimer, whose minister of communications I've been since 1981. Whatever the status of your health, you're still finding ways to help people solve the problems that they face, even if it takes a Westheimer Maneuver or two.

PORT ADELAIDE TO SHANGHAI

Taking Australia's game to the world

Andrew Hunter

with Tom Jonas and Michelangelo Rucci

Wakefield Press

Wakefield Press
16 Rose Street
Mile End
South Australia 5031
www.wakefieldpress.com.au

First published 2020

Cover designed by Stacey Zass
Edited by Julia Beaven, Wakefield Press
Typeset by Michael Deves, Wakefield Press
Printed in Australia by Ovato Book Printing, formerly Griffin Press, Adelaide

ISBN 978 1 74305 798 8

A catalogue record for this book is available from the National Library of Australia

Wakefield Press thanks Coriole Vineyards for continued support

For Sally, Theodore, Aurélien

Standing there on the embankment, staring into the current, I realised that – in spite of all the risks involved – a thing in motion will always be better than a thing at rest; that change will always be a nobler thing than permanence; that that which is static will degenerate and decay, turn to ash, while that which is in motion is able to last for an eternity.

From 'Flights', Olga Tokarczuk

Here, on the Great Wall
The snow, the sun, creation
Civilisation.

Andrew Hunter, 1 December 2015

Contents

Foreword

Tom Jonas

When someone asks me about playing a game of footy in China my natural response is 'I love playing there. We're undefeated.' Our three games in China have been an undisputed success on field; we've taken home the four premiership points each time. This answer feels superficial in respect to the club's investment and achievement in China. However, I think it's indicative of the way the whole of the Port Adelaide Football Club has embraced the challenge.

Our executive, led by Keith Thomas and the board of directors, could easily have re-invented a domestic business strategy, rehashing old plans and hoping for the best in a crowded market. Our sponsors could have put their dollars behind sporting teams in tried and tested markets, with significant and stable viewership. Our fans could have refused to travel to support the team, reasoning that it was too hard to traverse the globe to watch a game of footy. The players could have shouldered arms, complaining of the inconvenience, the heat, air quality, travel, and the time away from family, when the alternative was to play a simple away fixture in Victoria, where our record is nowhere as convincing.

I may be naïve, but from the moment Keith Thomas announced the plan to take the Port Adelaide Football Club to China I was 100% behind him. The way that Keith, Matthew Richardson and the team assembled beneath them approached the task inspired a sense of excitement, trust and possibility in what the club was setting out to achieve. It fitted with everything we were doing on the footy field under Ken. It was daring. We were taking the bull by the horns, taking it up to the rest of the competition rather than sitting and waiting for something to happen. Beyond the club, the naysayers were abundant, sprouting all of the reasons listed above and more against adopting such a bold strategy. This also appealed to the Port Adelaide spirit of not giving a shit what others thought, and not taking no for an answer. It was quintessential Port Adelaide, just in a different incarnation.

A variety of circumstances saw me exposed to the China engagement from early in its gestation. In 2013 I travelled to Hong Kong with Port Adelaide greats Tom Logan and Russell Ebert to host a junior footy clinic, be special guests at the Hong Kong Dragons AFL grand final luncheon, and present an agreement with the Hong Kong Football Club. The Hong Kong Football Club is located inside the infamous Happy Valley Racetrack in the heart of Hong Kong, which makes it an epic setting to kick a Sherrin around. While there were a few beers consumed on this trip, it was our first meaningful connection with Asia, and it felt significant to be part of it.

In 2016, a bad on-field indiscretion provided a small silver lining. It gave me the free time to travel to Asia with the PAFC board and China–Power Sponsor group to help launch our partnership with Chinese property company CRED. I saw this as an opportunity to help the club off field after I'd let down the club and couldn't do my job on it. We travelled to Guangzhou, Shanghai and Hong Kong where I represented Port Adelaide in a variety of ways which were challenging, uncomfortable, educational but, overall, very enjoyable. It was a crash course in Chinese culture and business culture. I found myself teaching the game to Chinese students, filming AFL street talk on Shanghai streets with people who had never seen our game before, mingling with high-net-worth Chinese businessmen (who likely had absolutely no idea who the hell I was), and being cajoled into performing a choreographed dance routine with a Chinese social influencer which would be beamed out to her tens of millions of weibo followers. Honestly, that dance, with my two left feet and the entire PAFC board watching on in amusement, was the biggest challenge of the trip. It's a miracle the playing group hasn't managed to get their hands on it yet.

This trip also exposed me to some of the individuals working tirelessly on the China Engagement team, and the sheer magnitude of grunt work needed to make it a success. Keith Thomas was the one with the bold vision, and the resolve to make it a reality. He's passionate, considered and a workaholic. Andrew Hunter is the General Manager of China Engagement. He too is a workaholic, very clever, a perfectionist and single-minded. Fortunately, the Huntsman saw something in me he liked, so we get along well. Louise Broadbridge is Executive Assistant to the CEO, Keith's right-hand man if you like. She makes sure everyone gets to the right place at the right time and knows what to do once they get there. I'm sure she's got me out of trouble once or twice. Promise Xu is a Chinese National working for Port Adelaide in Australia. She gave me a crash course in Chinese corporate culture and taught me some basic Mandarin, as well as essentially operating as a fixer while we were in Asia. Guangzhou local Chen Shaoliang was a gun footballer in China's ex-pat AFL league and moved to Australia to play for Port Adelaide. He embraced the challenge of moving across the world without knowing a word of English in the hope of making it at the top level. This speaks mountains of a man who has been an important advocate for Port Adelaide and the AFL in Australia and China. It was a privilege to work with all of these individuals and get a real-life perspective of the world outside of Australia and the AFL bubble.

The next China experience was different altogether. This time what felt like the whole Port Adelaide Football Club was in Shanghai to pull off the inaugural AFL game for premiership points in China. It was a 12-month build-up for the players, and a lot longer for some others. For this reason, the sense of expectation that as a playing group we 'do our bit' and perform was paramount. For what appeared a mundane regular fixture for most in the AFL world, actually felt like one of the most important games I'd ever played; and I know many others felt the same.

Despite 14 hours of overseas travel, the heat, and obvious cultural and logistical challenges our preparation was spot on. Spending five days acclimatising in China before the game served as a great opportunity to share time as a group, and also to explore Shanghai. There was a real buzz and genuine Aussie feel around the hotel, with a lot of family members, friends and amazing supporters having made the trip over for the game. This made Shanghai feel like home, and by the time the game rolled around everyone was ready to go.

In the rooms before the match you could cut the tension with a knife. It was obvious that the entire playing group recognised the importance of the game for reasons beyond just getting four premiership points; and just in case the significance hadn't hit home, Kenny made it crystal clear. The real evidence of this was in the changerooms after the game. We'd beaten the Gold Coast Suns convincingly, but regardless there was a collective sense of relief as everyone involved from players to coaches, the executive and Mr Gui of CRED enjoyed a celebratory beer.

China isn't the perfect place to play AFL, and I'm sure there have been hurdles along the way for Keith Thomas and his team. However, it's a worthy challenge and for me it isn't just about a game of footy. It's about being a part of something much larger. We have the opportunity as a collective to set Port Adelaide up for the long term. As players and administrators together, we can leave the Port Adelaide Football Club in a better place than we found it.

Introduction

Port Adelaide BC (Before China)

Michelangelo Rucci

Warren Tredrea, Port Adelaide Football Club's first AFL premiership captain, stepped out of a radio commentary box at Football Park at three-quarter time fearing his family football club was on the edge ... and ready to fall.

After 141 years of standing as Australia's most-successful football club – and the only club outside of Victoria to rise from suburbia to the national AFL competition – the Port Adelaide Football Club was 'bankrupt' in every sense. After 14 years in the big league, the football club was in crisis on and off the field.

That night, Port Adelaide was 98 points behind Collingwood (and there were still another 40 points to be hammered onto that deficit in the last term). It was not just the scoreboard that was troubling Tredrea, Port Adelaide's greatest goalkicker in AFL company. There was much more to concern him – and other Port Adelaide devotees.

Only 21,863 supporters had turned up at Football Park in Adelaide's western suburbs. It was Saturday night, the much-preferred timeslot for Port Adelaide fans. And this was one of the AFL's big drawcard opponents. Every club wants to host Collingwood for the crowds and television ratings these matches generate. This game remains the smallest gathering to a Port Adelaide vs Collingwood game, anywhere, anytime.

Only 21,863 had bothered to be at the decaying West Lakes arena to salute Tredrea's 2004 AFL premiership teammate Chad Cornes for his 239th and last AFL game for the Port Adelaide Football Club. This alone would have made Tredrea's heart sink.

The game was certain to end as Port Adelaide's eighth consecutive loss – and their 16th in 18 games of the depressing 2011 season.

Tredrea rang AFL media manager Patrick Keane wanting AFL chief executive Andrew Demetriou's private telephone number. He was to implore the league's boss that something had to be done at Alberton to save Port Adelaide from making a mockery of its century-old traditions – and worse.

'It was pathetic,' Tredrea recalls. 'And it was hard to watch as a former player. I knew the club had some issues financially and, for me, it was just rock bottom.'

And – even after Demetriou had reassured Tredrea that all would be fine at Port Adelaide – there was further despair to come. Season 2012 was another disaster, on and off the field. Senior coach Matthew Primus, one of the club's most-loved players, was sacked after defeat to the league's newest entry, Greater Western Sydney. Port Adelaide won just five of 22 home-and-away games to rank 14th of 18.

For Tredrea, the son of a Port Adelaide (SANFL) league player Gary, the demise of Port Adelaide as a competitive and respected team on the field was gut-wrenching. He had played during the 2001–2004 era in which Port Adelaide, despite its infamous chokes in the 2001–2003 top-eight final series, was a league pacesetter. It won two pre-season titles; the McClelland Trophy as the AFL's minor premier three times; and had a phenomenal 74-14 win-loss record in 88 home-and-away games.

From 2008 (after the grand final failure by a record 119 points to Geelong) to the end of 2012, Port Adelaide had a 34-75-1 win-loss-draw record in 110 games. There were no AFL finals appearances. In 2011, there were just three wins from 22 when Port Adelaide ranked 16th of 17, avoiding its first wooden spoon only by percentage.

And the picture was no better off the field.

Port Adelaide's home attendances at Football Park had peaked at the average of 31,845 in 2003. They fell to a record low of 19,911 in 2012 when the West Lakes arena had empty bays covered in tarps, impacting on the club's image. The six smallest crowds counted at Football Park for all AFL games were hosted by Port Adelaide during the darkest hours from 2010 to 2012. The lowest was 13,683 in the match against West Coast in 2012 when the club's future appeared lost to indifference among a frustrated and dejected supporter base.

Port Adelaide's AFL membership had reached a then-high 36,834 in the post-premiership glow of 2005. In 2010, this figure had fallen to a record low of 26,953. The club was bleeding with hefty losses and mounting debt, in 2010, a record operating loss of $3.69 million. Club chief executive Mark Haysman walked from his office on the eastern side of Alberton Oval to the playing field to stop training so he could update the players on the club's difficult position.

The SANFL, owner of the AFL licence sub-let to Port Adelaide, tired of repeatedly cutting bailout cheques at Alberton. It demanded the club strip its costs. The consequence was an under-funded football program, more bad results, more financial losses and more cuts. The vicious cycle rolled on and on with more disasters, on and off the field, making this Port Adelaide's darkest chapter in 15 years of AFL football.

There was discussion at AFL House. Modelling considered winding up the Port Adelaide Football Club and salvaging the AFL licence by rebadging the club as 'Central Australia Power', leaving the fresh-looking franchise to follow The Ghan's new railway tracks from Adelaide to Alice Springs to Darwin. There was even the prospect of Port Adelaide being relocated (and renamed) to satisfy Tasmania's desire for an AFL team.

Demetriou, one of the sharpest sporting administrators and businessmen to ever sit in the AFL's big office in Melbourne, did stay true to his promise to Tredrea. And, just as Port Adelaide was used as a pawn in 1990, the AFL once again used the Port Adelaide Football Club to achieve its 'ultimate solution' in Adelaide.

For more than 30 years, South Australia – or more to the point, the SANFL – had been a torment to the Victorian Football League's ambitions to be the game's national competition, the Australian Football League. Generally, the SANFL took exception to a national football competition being based in Melbourne, dominated by Victorian-based clubs and run by Victorians.

The SANFL had rejected the chance to be part of the VFL's expansion for 1987 when Western Australia opted to form the

West Coast Eagles. The VFL gave SA's spot to Brisbane with the Bears.

In 1990 the SANFL put any consideration of forming an AFL team on delay until 1993 – a decision the VFL–AFL could not accept. It needed to add South Australia to its national agenda, if only to appease its television backers with AFL games in every mainland state.

Port Adelaide broke this long-standing impasse between the SANFL and VFL masters – and was left at the altar by the AFL after Supreme Court injunctions were placed on Port Adelaide's ambitions. This forced the Victorians to look to the SANFL again and resulted in the conglomerate Adelaide Football Club, the Crows, ready for AFL action in 1991.

Port Adelaide was left to wait until 1997, after originally being pitched for AFL entry in 1996. And by 2012, after falling from the top of the AFL mountain, Demetriou used the 'Port Adelaide crisis' to solve all of its South Australian problems. Football was moved from the SANFL's outdated headquarters at West Lakes to return to a redeveloped Adelaide Oval, ending a 40-year cold war between the SANFL and SA Cricket Association.

The AFL removed the SANFL as the owner of the two SA-based AFL licences marked as 'Adelaide' and 'Port Adelaide'. Critically, the Port Adelaide Football Club was released from SANFL-cast irons that challenged the club's long-term future. It was free to find a new destiny in a new venue, Adelaide Oval, a ground rich in Port Adelaide successes before Football Park opened in 1974.

And Demetriou, on the morning of the 2012 AFL grand final,

sacked all but one member of the Port Adelaide Football Club board before entrusting No. 1 ticketholder and Sydney-based television personality David Koch as the club's new president.

Beyond a new home at Adelaide Oval, there was a new leadership group at Alberton, with full financing of the Port Adelaide football program. All this created new hope ... but the Port Adelaide Football Club still needed a business plan to ensure it could not only survive but thrive. And it needed new sources of financial support, particularly when Port Adelaide – despite the AFL badge on its jumper – could not get past the lobby to meet the marketing gurus of Corporate Australia. The failure to land a well-known major sponsor told of Port Adelaide's lack of appeal in the commercial world.

Within two years, Port Adelaide had looked beyond Australia. Port Adelaide fans were now excited about the future at the new Adelaide Oval and the announcements of key players signing new contracts. On 7 March 2014, during the club's season launch, Koch dropped into his speech the prospect of playing games in China.

Koch wanted Port Adelaide to play a pre-season trial match at the start of the 2015 season in Macau. Such a declaration hardly caused a ripple in the media – nor a follow-up story. Football in China, even for a practice game, seemed another far-fetched concept from a club president who savoured the 'showman' image. Few of the 400 Port Adelaide fans in the William Magarey Room at Adelaide Oval that night took note of the 'China Strategy'.

Rather than play a football game in China in March 2015, the Port Adelaide Football Club hired Andrew Hunter. And the ambitions in China changed dramatically – as did Port Adelaide's fortunes.

Port Adelaide to Shanghai: Taking Australia's Game to the World is the story of a proud football club that rose from the ashes of disaster to achieve in China landmark moments that other AFL clubs would have feared to dream.

In August 1989, a father and his two children shuffled off a Cathay Pacific aircraft into the stuffy night air. A strike had delayed their departure from London Heathrow, and the plane had been re-routed through Bahrain. The journey had been a long one. Finally, the family arrived in their hotel not far from Nathan Road, Hong Kong, and went straight to bed. A few hours later, his sister and father still soundly sleeping, the jet-lagged boy rose quietly, walked to the window of the hotel and looked out at the scene unfolding in the street below. On the road opposite, locals were preparing for market. Neon lights competed with passing bicycles, rickshaws and cars for his attention. Fish were being cleaned and gutted. He stood at the window transfixed, curious.

I want to see the world, he thought.

1 A brilliant teardrop from China's eye

Far in the East, like a brilliant teardrop from China's eye, there is a city like nowhere else ...

Clive James, *Postcard from Hong Kong*

Hong Kong is special to me. It was here my curiosity for different cultures was awakened. And twenty-five years later, it was Hong Kong that Port Adelaide considered as it looked for opportunities to engage in China, the Middle Kingdom.

Just a few weeks after I started as General Manager for Port Adelaide's community programs, I left for Hong Kong with other senior executives and board members, as well as South Australian football legends Bruce Abernethy and Graham Cornes, for a lunch to be held on 1 May 2015. For the second consecutive year, Port Adelaide had arranged a business lunch at the Hong Kong Football Club, a palatial establishment showcasing the British influence in Hong Kong. Although it was not my only visit to Hong Kong since my first trip there in 1989, it was an exciting moment – a moment in which another curiosity would be satisfied: how exactly was Port Adelaide going to realise its China dream?

It was easy to understand why Port Adelaide had looked first to Hong Kong in its desire to connect with China. Hong Kong, ceded by the Qing dynasty to the United Kingdom in August 1842, is a Special Administrative Region (SAR) of the People's

Republic of China. It was still in the hands of the UK when I first visited in 1989, before sovereignty was transferred in 1997 to Mainland China. All those year later, the bustle and the exotic smell (which I now knew was contributed to by pollution) remained.

Relative to most other Asian cities, Hong Kong is pretty easy to navigate for Westerners. For a footy club looking for a market beyond its national borders and natural comfort zone, it was as easy as any city in Asia. Outside London, Hong Kong has the largest number of resident Australians of any city in the world. Catching a taxi, ordering food, finding a pub where you can watch an AFL game, are all easy to do.

And among the 90,000-odd Australian residents in Hong Kong, there was a smattering of Port Adelaide loyalists – including John White and Peter Phillips. Each had made Hong Kong his home and built a successful career there, and both were now invited to help on our crazy adventure. Sam Koch, daughter of Port Adelaide Chairman David Koch, was also a long-time resident.

But Port Adelaide would not have contemplated the notion of developing business relationships in China had not Denis Way, a Vietnam veteran who had lived in Hong Kong since 1971, called the club in 2014. The club had publicly said it was open for business, and Denis suggested it have crack in China. Graham Cornes, in an article that appeared in the *Advertiser* in 2016, described Denis as 'ridiculously passionate'. That description is accurate.

Port Adelaide's engagement in China was commercially motivated. The sports industry in Australia is a highly contested space. There are around 90 professional sporting teams in Australia – about the same number as the United States, with its far larger population and economy. Port Adelaide is one of 18 AFL clubs, one of two in South Australia. The Adelaide Football Club is the other. South Australia is a relatively small state in terms of population and economy. Unwilling to tolerate the 'tarps' jibes of our cross-town rivals (in reference to the advertising used to cover bays at Football Park to hide the scarcity of the crowd), the club was determined to move away from its traditional place on the precipice of financial disaster.

New thinking was needed. Port Adelaide's audacious move into China is a South Australian story as much as it is an Australian story. Like South Australia, Port Adelaide had a modest domestic market and, as a South Australian club, is located far from the population and economic centres on the eastern seaboard. In modern professional sporting context, Port Adelaide is playing against the house. If it adopts a traditional, conservative approach, it will lose.

The strain of this reality was being keenly felt by 2012, when it was considered a basket case, unable to compete on or off the field. New thinking was required. It needed access to new markets. It needed to push through the traditional boundaries of what was considered possible. It needed to be open to the world.

New thinking can invigorate and inspire but turning the abstract into reality is not always easy. Port Adelaide was a quintessentially Australian organisation – which for our engagement in China would come to present both a challenge and an opportunity. For the moment, it was a challenge. And it was the reason why modest engagement in Hong Kong was as much daring as Port Adelaide could muster in the first instance.

Hong Kong was a mature market for Australian companies, with its Australian residents and established links. The business lunch was staged on Thursday 30 April 2015 at the Hong Kong Football Club (HKFC), an establishment that sits alongside, under and in the Happy Valley Racecourse and Hong Kong Jockey Club. A product of the colonial period, HKFC was founded to give British expats a place to play soccer and rugby. Now there is an indoor lawn bowls arena, pubs and restaurants, all in a palatial setting. But if the inside of HKFC is impressive, its outdoor grounds inside the perimeter of the racetrack are breathtaking. Looking up from the synthetic rugby pitches where the Hong Kong Sevens is played, it is difficult not to be struck by the size of the Jockey Club's pavilion in the foreground, or the high-rise buildings ringing the skyline.

Team China travelled from Guangdong Province to Hong Kong to play an abbreviated game prior to our business lunch. Their trip was sponsored by CLP Group (EnergyAustralia). The game was watched by the travelling luminaries Koch, Abernethy, Cornes and Keith Thomas. Team China arrived late, eventually took the field, and spent the next hour hiving around the ball, their enthusiasm evident but their feeling for the game largely absent.

The standard of play seemed to reflect the impossibility of the Port Adelaide dream to create a meaningful presence in China. In those early days, the mountain appeared high. Nonetheless, ANZAC Centenary Luncheon at HKFC generated some interest in the local Australian community. Denis paid

HK$21,000 at the auction, outbidding his son, to win two Port Adelaide playing shirts printed with the names of all senior footballers who served both their country and the club. One name on the list was Peter Chant, with whom Denis served in C Company, 9RAR. On the shirt, next to Peter Chant's name, was a symbol representing KIA, the car manufacturer.

The event was a success. The panel of speakers was well received, and the auction helped recoup the cost of holding the event, as well as contributing extra dollars to Team China. There were video highlights of the club's recent Anzac Day match against reigning premier Hawthorn, played in front of a packed Adelaide Oval and ending with a thrilling victory to Port Adelaide. Chairman Koch spoke of his ambition to play a pre-season game in China within a couple of years.

The club was flying at the time, on the back of an extraordinary turnaround and rapid improvements both on and off the field, so no one in the football community took him to task on this ambitious goal. But the event appeared almost to be designed to ensure that the local Chinese community would stay away.

Sure enough, there was only a handful of Chinese among the 277 attendees, which were almost entirely Australians and a few British who live locally. If an AFL team were to achieve a significant commercial outcome in Hong Kong, it probably would have happened already. The next step was to turn an idea into a strategy. And if Port Adelaide was to achieve the commercial outcomes it desired, it would need to venture out of its cultural comfort zone to the mainland where, at that moment, we had no presence and nothing to sell.

2 An intercultural Promise

To understand football is to understand Australia.

Heritier Lumumba

Footy clubs are unique places. There would be few other working environments in which the staff will collectively come to work Monday morning buoyant or mellow in mood. In 2015 expectation was high but results didn't follow. We lost to Fremantle away to open the season, then badly to Sydney in our first home game. After poor results, our CEO Keith Thomas – 'KT' – would make sure everyone was up and about, looking forward to the next week. He always knew what the supporters – including staff members – were feeling and, particularly back then, everyone responded to him.

When I arrived, Port Adelaide Football Club also appeared to reflect the early influences of modern Australia. For eight months I oversaw Power Community Limited (PCL), our excellent community arm offering nation-leading programs to support Aboriginal Australians staying in school and transitioning to work. These programs are led by the charismatic Paul Vandenbergh, the first Indigenous man to play in the NBL. The majority of members of the administration staff, however, had Anglo-Celtic origins. Its leadership team included executives bearing the names Richardson, Dawes,

McLeod, Thomas, Davies – and, now, Hunter. At least the name of our Human Resources General Manager, Simone de Laine, hinted at some Gallic flair.

This relative cultural homogeneity is not limited to employees. Excited by the task of helping develop a strategy to engage in China, I invited friend and local businesswoman Irena Zhang to attend Before the Bounce (BTB) for Port Adelaide's first home match of 2015, against Sydney. BTB is the Chairman's premium pre-game corporate event, which is attended by up to 500 significant partners and members. As I explained our aspirations to Irena, she looked wistfully around the room before noting that she was 'the only Asian face in the room'. It is reasonable to assert, then, that at the outset of our journey there was not a deep reservoir of intercultural understanding.

We were thoroughly outplayed that night, a portent of two seasons of unfulfilled promise. About halfway through 2015, as the club was struggling with on-field losses to Brisbane and Carlton (which effectively put an end to our finals aspirations) my belief that we needed to look to Mainland China, rather than continue to focus on Hong Kong, grew stronger. To do so, we needed to employ someone with bi-lingual skills.

This may have been a simple and necessary proposition on one level; on another it was groundbreaking. The AFL has often led social change – but it has just as often been reactive to broader social changes. I suspect that football clubs do not yet reflect the diversity of our society in terms of cultural background and gender – and certainly not sexual orientation. No listed AFL player has ever said they were gay.

The origins of football reflect the evolution of an Australian consciousness. (To be sure, the land now known as 'Australia' is timeless, but a consciousness of Australia as a unified nation among other nations, is not.) The sport we know as football absorbed both indigenous and British influences. The founder of the game, Tom Wills, was said to be raised in an Indigenous community and exposed to the game marngrook before he travelled to England to study at Rugby School. He ultimately returned from England to devise a game that captured elements of both rugby and the indigenous marngrook. This fusion of pre-colonial and colonial influences is written in the early evolution of the game.

(A mangrook was a ball made of possum skin, which was then stuffed. The day before the 2018 AFL grand final, commercial general manager James Lindsay and I met Rio Tinto's Managing Director in China, Ren Binyan. He was enthralled in the story, so I looked on the internet to see if it was possible to get my hands on one. Sure enough, someone by the name of Jim Poulter, who lived in the outer suburbs of Melbourne but had spent time in Indigenous communities, made them. The next morning, I took a taxi to his house, purchased one, and gave it to Binyan just before the match. He appeared both impressed and bemused in equal measure, saw one of the great grand finals, and eventually signed off on Rio Tinto's support for Shanghai 2019.)

Early on, then, football evolved in parallel with Australian society, and continues to reflect both positive and negative aspects of its character. Former Collingwood and Melbourne player Heritier Lumumba suggested in the documentary *Fair Game* that to understand football is to understand Australia. Football is still seen to be representative of Anglo-Celtic masculinity.

This is reflected in the ethos of its professional teams, by the media that interpret the games, and within the bosoms of its clubs. I saw discomfort in colleagues when I told them that I was vegetarian, it didn't score with a narrow view of what was 'normal'. 'That isn't Port Adelaide,' I was told. I can only imagine what it would be like for openly gay employees in the AFL industry.

A Chinese national employed at a footy club was just as uncommon. When we first employed Xu Nuo – known as 'Promise', her anglicised name, by most at the club – there was a level of discomfort in how to relate to a face not often seen in the inner sanctum of a professional club that plays 'Australia's game'. But Port Adelaide is an uncommon club. It has an uncommon idea of what can be achieved by a football club – one only has to look at the extent of its Aboriginal programs to see this.

This initiative was a beacon for those who wanted to be involved in something different. KT rallied supporters under the banner *Open to the World*. Chinese national Chen Shaoliang, an athlete from Guangdong Province with a basketball background who fell in love with Australian Rules football, was invited to wear its famous prison-bar jumper. In multicultural round, the players wore jumpers with their names displayed in Chinese characters. These initiatives piqued the members' curiosity in Chinese culture, language and history.

The fans were extremely supportive of what we were doing. Port Adelaide has the greatest fans, undeserving of the stereotyped image outsiders want to present. For multicultural round 2015, Chen Shaoliang and Zhang Hao, who assisted with game development in China, flew to Australia to take part in events that celebrate the game's diversity.

We played Western Bulldogs at Etihad Stadium that day. The team had strung some wins together, and it remained mathematically possible to make the finals. Expectations for this match were high. Port Adelaide, however, put in a stinker and the game was over by half-time. When Chen and Zhang said they wanted to leave the corporate box at half-time to sit with the fans, I hesitated, thinking the mood would be sombre. But we left together and walked around the concourse. In spite of these circumstances and the realisation that their season was over, Port Adelaide supporters approached Zhang and Chen, shaking hands and embracing them, welcoming them to Port Adelaide.

Still, we needed to work hard to make our Chinese friends feel welcome. Our sport, and our club, remained unfamiliar to Chinese people. A concerted effort to reach out was required. If footy clubs are to remain true to their traditional role of binding communities, they must continue to welcome and involve the community in all its diversity. At the time of writing, in a period of disruption due to COVID, some imagine it possible for Australia to turn inward, disengage from the rest of the world, return to a society insulated by migration, trade and investment policies. To believe this is possible is to ignore the rhythm of history. To wish for it is to reject the miracle of modern Australia. Our communities are diverse, our workplaces have evolved, and Australia is enmeshed with our neighbours in the region. When the COVID crisis is over, it will be in our interests to re-engage, and our sporting clubs should be part of this re-engagement. The successful clubs will be those that stay ahead of history's curve, rather than be the first down the slippery slide into the past.

We constantly played on this notion of Australian identity in our engagement with China. Football is a quintessentially Australian sport, we said. It provides a window into Australian culture. To learn about our sport is to become familiar with our values, our national culture, and our people. But there was still more to be done to ensure that football reflects a modern Australia, in all its dynamic diversity. And modern Australia could easily have built on early efforts to use our most popular sport to welcome new communities into the majoritarian, or mainstream, culture.

What comes as a surprise to many, however, is that football had helped bring Australia and Chinese people and governments together in the past. A strong anti-Chinese sentiment had taken hold in Victoria in the 1870s and 1880s. At an anti-Chinese rally held at the Melbourne Town Hall in 1880, attended by around 3000 people, Victorian Premier Graham Berry asked the audience: 'What is the point of having protection if we allow the wholesale immigration of an inferior race ...?' Despite this hostility, football played a role in bringing communities in Victoria together.

Nearby Ballarat had a thriving Chinese community during the goldrush. By 1890, the goldrush now over, Chinese either integrated into the community and found different work or returned home to China. The Chinese Goldfields Leagues started in Ballarat soon after. The first match, played between the Miners and the Gardeners on Friday 26 August 1892, attracted approximately 5000 spectators. Historian Robert Hess has argued that 'football was able to bring Chinese and European communities together and create a decade of tolerance and harmony across Victoria'.

As we will see later, many Chinese living in Australia returned to their homeland when the White Australia Policy was implemented in 1901 through the *Immigration Restriction Act*. There does not appear to have been an ongoing role for football as an instrument of engagement for Chinese communities in Australia thereafter. Until Port Adelaide.

The efforts made by Port Adelaide Football Club throughout 2015, in the context of a disappointing on-field performance, set the foundation for our initial success. Port Adelaide Football Club opened its arms to a new community – though more needs to be done – and its supporters backed the idea of the club engaging in China. The club decided to shift its strategy to Mainland China, with a view to engage Chinese companies with existing or developing interests in Australia.

In late 2015, five months after arriving at Port Adelaide, opportunity knocked.

3 Gui

Those who in ancient days were the best commanders
Were those who were delicate, subtle, mysterious, profound
Their minds too deep to be fathomed.

Lao Tzu, from the *Tao Te Ching*

The simplest starting point for any business strategy is surely to understand your assets – your strengths – and align them with a market that demands those assets. Clearly, it would be a long time before Port Adelaide could develop sporting assets of any value in China. Our greatest asset – our strength – was the incredible reach of the AFL in Australia. The trick was to identify Chinese companies or investors who would benefit from a stronger connection with Australia, and to explain the powerful role that sport plays in our society. It is difficult for Australian businesses to succeed in China – but just as difficult for Chinese businesses in Australia, particularly when involved in high-profile or politically sensitive investments.

Throughout 2015, we therefore looked to identify Chinese investors and businesses that would benefit from a deeper engagement through sport. In August, we organised with the South Australian Government to host a group of migrant investors and their intermediaries at a home match against Greater Western Sydney. At the time, we were concerned that the game against GWS would be a fizzer, one-sided and lacking spectacle. How times have changed.

The match against GWS took place on 15 August 2015. Would not beat them again until the 2020 season. But we won that day. Best on ground was Brendon Ah Chee, who polled three Brownlow Medal votes. Like Jake Neade, Ah Chee has a grandfather from southern China. A good omen? We made some important connections at the event, co-hosted by Premier Weatherill. Someone by the name of Loretta Lai was in the room.

I met with Loretta the following week. She spoke about several clients of hers and arranged to introduce me to one at a dinner to be held on 4 September 2015 at Citi Zen restaurant. It was here that I met Gui Guojie, Chairman of Shanghai CRED Real Estate, and invited him to attend Port Adelaide's final match of the season against Fremantle, the following day. Much work was done overnight to better understand his company and his business interests. The next morning, I struggled to explain to colleagues, tired from a long season and preparing for a home match, how big an opportunity this could be. I couldn't even convince a colleague to drive from his home in nearby Henley to Alberton to get a boxed guernsey to give as a gift! But opportunities like this don't come along often so I called upon my (then) part-time colleague, Promise, to help pull everything together.

A Port Adelaide guernsey with number eight on the back was prepared in an appropriate gift box with a personal translated message placed inside. KT gave Gui a tour of the change rooms before the game. He was enthralled by the sport, the crowd and the occasion. Every time Hamish Hartlett, who wore the number eight jumper Gui had been gifted earlier, touched the ball, Gui jumped up to high-five those around him.

Interestingly, he also immediately understood the game, which is uncommon for those who were not raised watching the sport. When, 20 minutes into the second quarter, Port Adelaide's enigmatic crowd favourite John Butcher rose above the pack to take a spectacular mark, the crowd – including Gui – rose as one. Throughout his career, Butcher had struggled with set shot conversion and he had already missed at least three shots at goal on the day. As the crowd settled, I saw Gui speaking to his translator alongside him and I asked what he had said. 'I don't know why everyone is so excited,' came the response, 'he will miss the goals anyway ...' Within an hour of his first-ever match, Gui understood the game and the tendencies of the players. (Ironically, the maligned Butcher kicked the goal from 50 metres out at an angle, drawing a euphoric response from his teammates and the crowd.)

It was hard not to warm to Gui. Tactile, particularly when compared to most Chinese, he had an infectious smile and loved to hug. When I travelled to China to discuss a potential partnership in November 2015, knowing that I was a vegetarian, he took me to eat with the monks at the monastery in Shanghai he financially supports. He welcomed me into his home and cooked a vegetarian meal. For someone so time poor, he was incredibly generous and warm. He was also a visionary and prepared to take risks.

Although not announced until 14 April 2016, Shanghai CRED Real Estate Co. formally became a sponsor of Port Adelaide Football Club on 29 February 2016. The agreement between the two parties was signed in Shanghai at 2:20 pm, the traditional starting time of the SANFL games, of which KT played 332 league matches. It was a special moment for the club, and wonderful to share it with KT. But its announcement evoked mixed reactions at home, where the achievements were seen in a highly politicised context.

The Australian media initially linked the sponsorship with CRED's involvement in a bid for the purchase of the vast network of cattle stations owned by S. Kidman & Co. When that sale was blocked by the Commonwealth, it was anticipated that the sponsorship would be somehow annulled. The *Australian Financial Review* (AFR) asked whether Gui's 'sudden passion for AFL might wane', referring to rumours circulating in Melbourne that this may be the case. The local newspaper, the *Advertiser*, questioned whether the Foreign Investment Review Board's (FIRB) rejection of the bid would impact the three-year sponsorship arrangement between CRED and Port Adelaide. After the first FIRB rejection, there were concerns within the club that we would suffer great embarrassment. The sponsorship agreement had been signed but the money was yet to be received. With the single bank cheque for a seven-figure partnership came much relief.

Several Australian journalists struggled to understand why someone from China would financially commit to an Australian football – as opposed to a soccer – club. To demonstrate any motivations other than those he articulated would, however, be difficult.

If Gui viewed Port Adelaide simply as an avenue through which he could facilitate investment in Australia, he had found a willing partner in Port Adelaide. Our strategy was predicated on helping Chinese companies deepen their engagement with the Australian people – in the same way that Toyota, a

Japanese company, has used football. And in 2016 and 2017, CRED's engagement attracted popular interest in Australia, and helped our project attract the support of government and businesses, both in Australia and in China.

Our strategy, based on an understanding of our strengths and weaknesses, was different to other Australian sporting entities engaged in China. We couldn't replicate the facile business-to-consumer approach of most sporting clubs, as we had no resonance in China. We believed we had a more sophisticated offering.

The negative commentary in the media infers that the partnership between Port Adelaide and CRED was instrumentalist. It suggests that the partnership was designed to meet a short-term imperative: a relationship driven by CRED's need to attain a social licence to operate in Australia (consistent with the club's initial claims of promoting the potential benefit it could bring to Chinese businesses). KT said in an interview with John Stensholt of the *Australian Financial Review* (AFR) that Port Adelaide wanted to 'appeal to companies that are looking to break into Australia and promote their brand' or invest in Australia. In another interview, he remarked that 'because we play on the national stage, we feel [we are] a great vehicle for Chinese businesses to enter Australia ...' Our commercial ambition appeared naked at times, even if cloaked in the rhetoric of friendship. We believe strongly in the intrinsic beauty of what we were doing – creating better understanding and engagement between the peoples of Australia and China. But we were also millions of dollars in debt, and the club's decision to engage in China was commercially motivated.

Gui's immediate interest in the game did not mean that he continued to closely follow the fortunes of Port Adelaide from afar. In May 2016, a meeting was held soon after he had paid the first million dollars of a three-year, one-million-dollar-per-season, agreement. Port Adelaide's season was in the balance having won four of its first seven matches including three heavy defeats to GWS, Adelaide and Geelong. At home, tension caused by concern over the team's performances was palpable. The meeting was held in a room set in a formal squared horseshoe formation. Gui arrived and sat down. 'So,' he said through a translator, 'has the season started yet?'

Gui never coupled football sponsorship with other business interests in Australia. We took at face value his words, often quoted in the media, where Gui described how he was moved by the sport. To the media, he spoke of how his 'inner passion came alive' upon watching his first match at Adelaide Oval and seeing three generations of supporters enjoying the game together, and stated that his 'reunion with a real game has once again (relit) the enthusiasm for sport which was buried in (my) heart'.

His experience was also in sharp contrast to the spectator experience at soccer games in China; as we will see, the Shanghainese authorities also assumed soccer and football supports to be cut from the same cloth. Gui, however, immediately understood that in Australia, football 'was no longer merely a sport; the experience transcends into a lifestyle, and that's the most charming part of sports culture: creating an enjoyable and exciting atmosphere for people to experience and participate in'. Gui later described his motivation for bringing football to China as a chance to improve the standard of life of his fellow countrymen, as he described in another interview, 'by watching a world-class sport and learning about Australian culture'. He repeatedly described his support for football as his 'gift to China'.

I did not doubt that Gui understood that his association with our most popular sport could positively impact his business interests. And I was comfortable with that because for me, the chance to use sport to develop greater intercultural understanding outweighs concerns over the right level of foreign investment for Australia – concerns that surely would have been less acute had, say, a European company wished to purchase the Kidman cattle stations.

I was, however, becoming increasingly uneasy with his plans to live export Australian cattle to abattoirs in Shandong Province, China; abattoirs that would have no experience of killing such large beasts. Contrary to the line adopted by the industry and echoed by most politicians, the industry kills jobs that could be created in Australian abattoirs, where animal welfare standards are higher, and in value-adding industries like packaging.

But in the private sector, the profit motive is often more powerful than any individual's ethical position. I wrote a note to Gui, who contributed money to monasteries and occasionally waxed lyrical about his Buddhist convictions, about the Buddhist tradition of *fangsheng*, the practice of purchasing animals due for slaughter and releasing them. In China, devout Buddhists don't harm animals or eat meat. I eventually sent the letter, with a cover note, in 2020, once I had ceased to work at Port Adelaide. For almost five years, I kept it in the front of my diary, an albatross around my neck.

I also had a strong sense that the bilateral relationship between Australia and China needed more than cultural understanding. It had become mired in tensions over foreign investment, larger geo-strategic questions, and seen as part of a zero-sum game with the United States. There needed to be a moment, mutually positive and unthreatening, that could capture the imagination of the Australian people, our fascination for the country, its people and history. Our engagement in China deserved to be elevated to a position that went beyond sport, beyond business. It was a potential that needed to be understood and seized. Little did we know the extent to which the bilateral would deteriorate in the years that followed.

Gui's contribution to Port Adelaide does not get the consideration it deserves. The initial three-year agreement has been extended by a further five years. That, with his annual contribution to the game played in China, makes him the most significant financial supporter in the club's history. Strangely, few people acknowledge, let alone celebrate this reality.

On 1 March 2016, the day Shanghai CRED Real Estate Stock Co. and Port Adelaide Football Club signed a three-year sponsorship agreement, we went to a restaurant to celebrate. There was much to feel positive about – the strategy was simple and confined, the benefit for the club significant, and the costs and risk associated with the strategy low. The mood was ebullient, the toasting frequent and heart-felt.

Amid the merriment, Gui leant across to me and, in full voice, said: 'I want your prime minister to be involved. He needs to come to Shanghai so that we can talk to him about our plans to bring football to China.' Yes, of course, no problem. Gui was serious. KT was laughing at my discomfort. How the hell are we going to do that? Six weeks later, it happened.

4 The announcement

An enormous field, extraordinary athleticism, it is the leaping, jumping, flying game …

Prime Minister Malcolm Turnbull, 14 April 2016

On 13 April 2016, I arrived at Adelaide Airport at around 4:30 am to board CX173 to Hong Kong, and then travel on to Shanghai. The next day, the Prime Minister was due to announce Port Adelaide's desire to play a match for premiership points in China in 2017. This event was the culmination of six-weeks of effort, brilliance and extraordinarily good fortune. It would take our engagement in China to a whole new level. But I had never felt so distracted, distraught, or full of self-loathing.

Many people who work at football clubs operate in close proximity to their heroes, but I have attempted to avoid vicarious tendencies in which my happiness depends on the successes and failures of others. I may never have understood the clamour to be around those in the public light, or let my feelings peak and trough based on the exploits of others, but nonetheless I succumbed to the classic fantasy of falling in love with, and then marrying, my heroine.

I met Sally in 2006 at the Australian Institute of Sport. Sally comes from a family of swimmers. Her great-aunt competed at the 1936 Olympic Games in Berlin, and her family are coaches at Central Aquatic Swim Club in Perth. I was in the final throes of my underwhelming career as a professional athlete and was immediately smitten. The next decade was spent following her wonderful swimming career. I watched Sally at the Olympic Games in Beijing and London, and at the Commonwealth Games in Glasgow, where she won an individual silver medal. A year earlier, in 2013, I watched Sally on television, when she won another silver medal at the World Championships in Barcelona.

Swimming is in Sal's blood, and her career on the national team spanned almost the entirety of our relationship. When I returned to Australia after seven years in Europe, I lived in Canberra so we could be together. Following the London Olympics, we moved to Adelaide with our two dogs, Leo and Tolstoi. At this point, Sally made two important decisions: first, to continue swimming, but also to aim to medal at the next Olympics. To do so, she wanted to focus on the 100-metre breaststroke, which carried with it the opportunity to make the strong Australian medley relay team. The courageous decision was vindicated early, when Sally became national champion in both the 100 and 200 metres breaststroke in 2013 and medalled at the World Championships. But as she got deeper into the Olympic cycle, it became clear there was going to be serious competition.

The 2016 National Championships – which doubled as the Olympic Trials – were held at the Marion pool, the home of Sally's new swimming club in Adelaide. On Saturday night, Sally swam a personal best time but just missed the team for the 100 metres. Complete devastation. There remained one chance to make the team: the 200 metres final on Tuesday night. Again, Sally came up just short. Only an athlete understands how that moment – that painful last moment when you know it's all over – hurts. In Sally's case, the pain was enormous. She had made a courageous decision, and come so close to vindicating it, but it was not to be. There were many tears but little sleep the night following that race. I left for China in the early hours of the following morning. It was 13 April. Sally's birthday.

Six weeks earlier, we had started working to get the Prime Minister involved in our Chinese ambition. The only chance I could see was to do something around Australia Week in China (AWIC), which was imminent. AWIC was a biennial event traditionally organised by Austrade that attracts senior government representation, often including the PM and trade minister. We knew that Prime Minister Turnbull was planning to attend with a significant business delegation from Australia. Would he do something around our engagement in China?

We first tested the waters with the head of Austrade in China, Michael Clifton. Only a few weeks after Gui had casually asked us to invite the Australian Prime Minister to Shanghai, KT, Promise and I were sitting in front of Michael in the Austrade offices in the CITIC building in Nanjing Road West, not far from our hotel. Michael confessed his love for the Bombers, apologised for the club's parlous state (apology accepted) and confirmed that Prime Minister Turnbull was planning to come to Shanghai as part of AWIC. He said the PM's trip would be anchored around two key meetings, but there may be an opportunity for a signing ceremony to be scheduled around these anchor points. There were other announcements proposed, he said, but none as elevated as ours. There were some logistical issues to overcome, but we left the meeting thinking it would happen.

At that moment, it felt like anything was possible. There were great expectations for the season, which had yet to begin, and, off field, what had appeared crazy now appeared perfectly reasonable. I contacted Frances Adamson, International Advisor in the office of the prime minister, upon my return to Australia. Australian Ambassador to China until 2015, Frances offered encouragement and guidance. It was Austrade's program, she said, and we should continue to work closely with them. As someone who studied at an international relations school, it was a thrill for me to talk to diplomats, and there is no one more impressive, more thorough or more professional than Frances. And each step of the way, we were encouraged to believe that it was possible our announcement could be part of the PM's program.

We had been given hope that our announcement could be included on the official program, but what would we announce? There were some uninspiring options. We could revisit the already signed agreement with CRED, so that Gui would have a reason to be involved. We could announce our plans to develop a school footy program in China, or say something about our recent agreement with China Central Television (CCTV). But I was not sure that these initiatives, which had already been announced in some form, would be enough. A compelling argument for the Prime Minister's involvement needed something more.

Kochie had for a while been talking publicly about our ambition to play a game in China. These statements were a good way to capture the imagination of a public struggling to imagine how the future for PAFC in China would look. Was it even possible to play an official game in China? There had been an exhibition game in 2010, but an official game would take considerably greater effort. Even so, we came to the view that we would need to announce our intention to play a game for premiership points if we were to attract Turnbull during such an auspicious and historic moment in his prime ministership.

The season began unconvincingly with a win at home against St Kilda, followed by a heavy defeat in the Showdown, which complicated the monumental events unfolding away from the public eye. We were by this stage in contact with the political advisors and bureaucrats piecing together the detail of the PM's schedule, which we were told would include our announcement. Keith Thomas's EA, Louise Broadbridge, worked with them on the detail of the announcement, which was initially planned to be part of a larger event arranged by Tourism Australia. Then, in the week leading up to the event, we were told that our announcement would be a stand-alone event – the first on Prime Minister Turnbull's schedule, on his first trip to China as PM.

As someone deeply interested in international affairs, and the history of the Sino-Australian relationship, I felt excited knowing that Port Adelaide's engagement in China was considered worthy of such a moment. Even in this moment of domestic politics coming before all other considerations, I remain convinced that leaders consider carefully how such historic moments in their careers will echo through time. Discussions that took place on the first visits to China of other prime ministers had not been trivial affairs. Gough

Whitlam, on his first trip to China as prime minister, arrived in Beijing at 2 pm on 31 October 1973, and was received by Premier Zhou Enlai in the Great Hall of the People at 5 pm for his first official engagement. Turnbull arrived in Shanghai at 6 am on 14 April 2016, and in the Peace Hotel at 8:05 am endorsed Port Adelaide's desire to play an AFL match in China the following year.

Four days after Port Adelaide defeated a depleted Essendon – a team rendered unrecognisable from the previous season by WADA's recent decision to suspend most of its players for taking banned supplements – and the night after Sally's world fell apart, a small team of Port Adelaide executives and *Advertiser* journalist Michelangelo Rucci left for Shanghai. Morose and guilt-ridden, I maintained my own counsel, spoke to Sal on the phone, and tried to write a few opening remarks, as I would MC the event. In transit in Hong Kong, affairs started to unravel. Our flight to Shanghai was delayed by a couple of hours and as we sat in the Cathay Pacific lounge, our attention turned to the backlog of flights. Our Chairman's flight from Sydney had not yet arrived. And flights later in the evening had been cancelled.

We boarded our last flight not knowing if Kochie would make it. Upon our arrival in Shanghai, his participation in the event looked distinctly unlikely. This, we knew, would be mortifying to him. There were also practical considerations – he was a signatory to the memorandum of understanding that the PM would witness. So, we arrived in Shanghai deep into the night, and spent the next hours scrambling for a solution. The staff at the Portman Ritz Carlton were, as usual, wonderfully accommodating of our requests. The paper they offered was not ideal, but the quality of the paper that would be signed did not seem important. Port Adelaide was going to be written into a page in the history of the bilateral relationship.

I started each day I was in Shanghai with a 30-minute run down Nanjing Road West, to clear the mind and awaken the body (a routine I didn't break across 45 trips to China with PAFC). We arrived at the Peace Hotel early, watching over the last-minute preparations. The Peace Hotel is located on Nanjing Road East, not far from our hotel. Built by Sephardic Jew Sir Victor Sassoon in the 1920s, it offers beautiful views of the Bund. We were familiar with the hotel because one month earlier, in the jazz bar on the ground floor, KT, Louise, Loretta and I had celebrated the signing of the agreement with Shanghai CRED. An old jazz band, immortalised in the film *As Time Goes By*, still plays there every night. And KT still mocks me for taking him to that jazz bar ... I guess it wasn't a Port Adelaide thing to do.

I would like to say that there were stunning views on that clear spring morning, but in truth the skyline was ruined by a thick layer of pollution. Despite this, the view from the balcony remained impressive, and as the room used for the signing began to fill with journalists and government officials, it was not pollution but excitement that filled the air. A beautiful, golden mural had been mounted on the wall behind the signing table, and the flags of both countries completed the scene. As eight o'clock approached, the journalists formed a large pack in their designated area, and the Prime Minister entered the room.

A positive energy swept into the room with the Prime Minister, who was nearing the end of his brief political honeymoon. With David absent, Port Adelaide was represented by Keith Thomas. AFL Chief Executive Officer Gillon McLachlan was there, as was Gui. In the audience was also South Australia's Minister for Investment and Trade, Martin Hamilton-Smith. Silence descended on the room, I looked to KT who nodded, and the proceedings started. I had 90 seconds to kick things off which, considering it took 40 seconds to complete the formal acknowledgements, wasn't a lot of time. Following the acknowledgements, I mentioned that there had never 'been a more exciting time to be an Australian bringing AFL to China', in what was supposed to be a cheeky reference to Turnbull's ongoing assertion that there had never been a more exciting time to be an Australian. To his credit, he smiled and then ran with the same formula of words in his remarks.

Turnbull was upbeat. He called Aussie Rules the 'most exciting football code'. This was controversial enough, sure to annoy fans of every other football code, but the PM was only just warming up. 'An enormous field, extraordinary athleticism, it is the leaping, jumping, flying game ...' The PM was clearly enjoying the moment. Then he declared that Port Adelaide would play a game in China in 2017. The words 'best intentions', or any other words that softened the commitment, were notably absent. This put the AFL in a difficult spot, as no one could really know whether it would be possible to play an official game the next year. We were on the hook now.

After the PM had left, KT gave a number of interviews and photos. It was a genuinely positive occasion, even if some of the hard-nosed journos insisted on asking Gui how the announcement related to his interests in Kidman. But that was expected, and nothing could detract from the pleasure of the moment. Journalist Michelangelo Rucci, who had supported Port Adelaide from childhood, had a twinkle in his eye. KT, who had invested so much in the strategy, was thrilled. It was a memorable and historic moment. But the hard work had just started – and would be completed in the context of a very challenging 2016 season on the field.

5 CCTV

I want to fly home, riding the air
But I fear the ethereal cold up there, the jade and crystal mansions are so high.

Su Shi

The match that had preceded the announcement in Shanghai, against Essendon at Adelaide Oval, was historic. Port Adelaide opened with a blistering first quarter, kicking seven goals to one, effectively deciding the outcome of the game. The rest of the game did not reach the same heights – at least from a Port Adelaide perspective – which was unfortunate as it would be one of the most watched games in the season. It was the first game of Australian football broadcast on CCTV, the largest television network in the world.

Five months earlier, our media GM Daniel ('Norts') Norton, Promise and I travelled to Beijing to meet with Zhang Bin, the director of sport for CCTV and the most famous sports commentator in China. We were travelling with Port Adelaide's Aboriginal Academy side on its tour to China (another important step in our engagement of China) but left the group to take the overnight bullet train from Guangzhou to Beijing, arriving to a crisp morning at the beginning of a Beijing winter.

Two Billion Eyes, the title of a book on the history of CCTV, written by Zhu Ying, gives some sense of the station's significance. From the early days of the People's Republic of China, the media was considered a mouthpiece of the state, and CCTV an important link between the Chinese Communist Party and the people. It was subsidised by the state from 1958 to 1979, when commercials were introduced. During the 1990s, subsidies decreased rapidly and the need for commercialisation through advertising revenues increased accordingly. Today, CCTV must therefore meet an important commercial imperative. It effectively serves three masters: the party state, the market, and the public. It is a significant institution.

And when it comes to sport on CCTV, Zhang Bin is the man. Main anchor of all the major sports events broadcast on CCTV, including the Olympics, the World Cup and European Championships, Zhang Bin is one of the most recognisable faces in Chinese sport. At 193 cm, he is tall for a Chinese. Born and raised in Beijing, in some ways he reflects the character of his home town: honest, larger-than-life, and self-assured. There was no pretence when dealing with Zhang Bin.

We had agreed to meet him for lunch at a vegetarian restaurant. On the train the night before, Norts, Promise and I had discussed a strategy for the conversation, which we hoped would ignite CCTV's interest in Port Adelaide and the AFL. As soon as lunch started, however, Promise and Zhang Bin enjoyed a lengthy dialogue in Mandarin. Promise's enthusiastic (and incessant) chatter with a man I described to others as 'the Bruce McAvaney of Chinese sport' was a departure from the script – but understandable when one considers the role that CCTV plays in China, and the stature of the man with whom we were eating lunch.

The meal was a great joy. The conversation flowed well. Zhang Bin and Norts made comparisons between the AFL and the Chinese Super League, and I was happy to hear that Zhang Bin's favourite sport was volleyball (I had played professionally in Europe and a few games for Australia, back in the day). We gave him a boxed Port Adelaide jumper that had been used in the previous season's multicultural round, and by the end we felt we had established a connection. More importantly, he appeared interested in the product we were pitching to him and asked that we send him an inventory of products that he could consider for the following season.

The following day, we took the Aboriginal Academy side to the Great Wall. It was bitingly cold. The sky was clear and the landscape, visible from our privileged vantage point, was covered by a thin sheet of snow. KT had arrived in Beijing that morning to join the final two days of the tour, conducting interviews on the Great Wall in a Port Adelaide polo shirt. The Aboriginal Academy performed their war dance in front of bemused bystanders, for the purpose of a story that would run on page three of the *Australian* the next day.

When I look back on the five years at Port Adelaide, I see this moment most vividly, but at the time I was so obsessed by achieving the club's commercial endgame that I did not appreciate the beauty of the moment. A photo of this team on the Great Wall occupied a prominent place in my office. When one of the Academy boys, Kieran Agius, tragically died in 2019, it reminded me life is too precious, too unpredictable, too ephemeral, to feel anything other than gratitude for moments like this.

The impressive sight of this team of young Aboriginal

footballers performing their war dance on such an iconic monument, many thousand kilometres from home, piqued new thinking. What if we didn't simply try to pitch games of football to CCTV, or highlights shows, but also something that uses the sport as a platform for a broader story of cultural exchange and understanding? The idea of a documentary about Chen Shaoliang (who was due to train with Port Adelaide the following season) and his experience training with Port Adelaide was born.

A flurry of exchanges with CCTV ensued. With the season approaching, time was not on our side – but there was a willingness to do something significant together. We wanted to appeal to the three masters that CCTV served – the party state, the market and the public – and tailored our offering accordingly. We stressed both the exciting nature of the sport, as well as its potential to contribute to mutual understanding and world harmony (*hexie shijie*) – an admittedly outdated political slogan that had in the past been commonly used by the Chinese Government. Harmony is only possible when disparate things come together in a pleasing way, and we wanted to share a unique aspect of Australian culture with China, for mutual benefit and understanding.

These messages were well received and, on 3 March 2016, Port Adelaide and CCTV reached a handshake agreement on the broadcast of a weekly documentary show on Chen's experience in Adelaide as well as AFL game highlights, along with full broadcasts of two matches early in the season. It was more than we had originally expected. As the conversation developed, CCTV asked about the broadcast of matches. It moved quickly, exceeded expectations, and the conversations were successfully concluded two days after we signed the commercial agreement with CRED.

CCTV developed their own team of in-house football 'specialists', as it was not possible to source commentators or experts from elsewhere. CCTV insist on a particular voice and tone for its presenters, with many of its commentators and news readers employing a similar style and intonation. When Promise heard CCTV's commentary of Port Adelaide's game against Essendon, it recalled the television voices of her youth.

Port Adelaide appreciated how special it was to work with CCTV to allow China to access our most popular national sport. In an email she sent to convey her excitement, Promise said that the feeling she had when securing a partnership with CCTV reminded her of a poem of Su Shi, one of the greatest poets of the Song dynasty, in which the poet states: *'I want to fly home, riding the air/But I fear the ethereal cold up there, the jade and crystal mansions are so high!'* These were halcyon days, anything felt possible. This feeling carried us a long way.

It took a long time to receive the audience numbers from CCTV, but we were satisfied when we did. Using a complicated formula, which extrapolated the audience size in certain cities and applied them across the country, we found that the delayed broadcast of Port Adelaide's Friday night home match against Essendon had approximately 2.12 million views. But this outcome was exceeded by the second match, which was broadcast live to a reported audience of 3.87 million, making it the most watched home-and-away match in the history of the sport.

We were often frustrated by the lack of support we received

from the AFL. Our desire to provide material they could use to promote the weekly broadcasts invariably came at a cost, which was borne by Port Adelaide. The AFL was reluctant to promote the audience achieved through these broadcasts. We found these attitudes inexplicable but punched on.

When I informed an AFL executive of the unique opportunity CCTV presented, and argued that no other sporting body, including the NBA and NHL, were broadcast on CCTV without first incurring a significant cost, the veracity of this was questioned. From 2017, AFL negotiated various arrangements with Guangzhou TV, Shanghai Media Group, Ten Cent and BesTV. Each came at a significant cost. The CCTV partnership remains a highlight of this journey.

The audience peaked in the second half of the game against Geelong, as our opponents pulled away in front of an increasingly impatient home crowd. This was not ideal. The early reaction to the broadcasts, however, was deeply pleasing. Indeed, the initial popularity encouraged CCTV to seek an agreement to broadcast weekly matches throughout the 2016 season.

But even more exciting was the production of the documentary, an enormously time-consuming venture that was only possible due to the incredible support of the state government, as well as an intense collaboration between our media team and local film company, 57 Films. Norts worked tirelessly on this project. The combination of the weekly broadcasts and the documentary series provided a package that reflected our belief that sport was an underused vehicle for intercultural understanding and deeper relations. It took our club, and our sport, to the most populous country in the world.

In an interview with Angus Grigg from the AFR, KT shared his belief that the 'partnership with CCTV is more than just entertainment; it is about understanding. Through our regular AFL programs on CCTV, the viewers in China will see more of Australia and learn more about our culture and Australian life'. Just as Aussies who followed football became more interested in China through our engagement program, a nascent audience in China had the chance to learn more about our culture through our most popular sport.

Such esoteric considerations get short thrift from the media and supporters when things don't go as they should on the field – and our season was unravelling fast. Even before the heavy defeat to Geelong, the announcement in Shanghai was followed by a crushing loss to Greater Western Sydney in Canberra. Following this 86-point defeat, the back-page headline of the *Advertiser* screamed 'Digging a hole to China'.

The easy accusation that the club was distracted, its off-field success coming at the price of on-field performance, would test the club's resolve. It would be a question of leadership.

6 Leadership

Well, we don't know what is behind this waterfall. If one of us is brave enough to go find out, then why don't we accept him as our King?

Wu Cheng'en in *Journey to the West*

By June 2016, when Port Adelaide lost to bottom-placed Fremantle by 17 points in Perth, it was clear we would not play finals football. But the idea that those responsible for the team's performance would somehow be distracted by an off-field interest in China was, in my opinion, strange. The club had been conscious of the risks of this perception festering, during a season in which the playing performance did not meet its own high expectations. Club Chairman David Koch and CEO KT remained steadfast in their support of our engagement in China.

When confronted with the reality of committing to a match in China – and the costs and complexities associated with it – KT and Kochie remained effusive and would not countenance equivocation. The game in Shanghai that would ultimately be played in May 2017 wouldn't have been possible without strong leadership during those long winter months of 2016, when wins against mid-ranking teams Collingwood, Melbourne and North Melbourne were balanced by losses to premiership contenders Hawthorn and Greater Western Sydney. On-field momentum remained elusive.

Not all stakeholders, including members of the AFL Commission and PAFC board, were steadfast in their support but, throughout it all, the Chairman and CEO showed leadership in not letting the immediate distract from the agreed strategy. The inspiration behind their commitment to strategy came from different sources. For KT, Port Adelaide's engagement in China was rational, for Kochie there was also an emotional element.

Kochie had described his father, Dean, as his hero, his role model and his compass. Dean, who died in 2009, exported coal to China at a moment in history when few Australians were doing business in the Middle Kingdom, and I think David saw Port Adelaide's engagement in China as his own contribution to the history of the bilateral relationship. Australians doing business with China in Dean's era would have been as rare as footy club presidents in the present era looking to play a game in China for premiership points.

KT had a rational explanation as to why this was important to explore. He often explained that even when Port Adelaide was successful on the field, as a club competing for over a century in the SANFL, or in its more recent life as an AFL club, it had struggled to be commercially viable off it. And when Port Adelaide struggled on field, its business model broke down completely. He believed that Port Adelaide needed to seek new opportunities, without losing focus on the heartland. Engagement in China on one level appeared irrational; on another it made perfect sense. Port Adelaide was in need of new markets and investments, and needed to look beyond its postcode, beyond the state's borders and, perhaps, beyond Australia.

Approval by the AFL commission and Port Adelaide board for an in-season match in China required more than vision. Rightly, the AFL wished to preserve its image, and understood the potential risks of playing a match in China. It demanded that a commercial model and government approvals were in place before it would publicly commit to the match. Port Adelaide needed to ensure that the game in Shanghai would not lead to financial loss. Knowing the draw would be released in October, we were working against the clock to provide these assurances.

Was it important to play a match in China? There was no obligation to do so. Remember, the original objective of the club was for our engagement in China to yield one major sponsorship, a sponsorship that would bring a new revenue stream of at least a million dollars. This was achieved within a relatively short period of time – and without great risk and with high yield, as only two staff members were at that time working on the strategy.

It took courage, conviction and vision to take the dividend of this initial success and use it to invest in a longer-term strategy that had the potential to yield a more substantial commercial outcome. And, of course, we were encouraged by Gui, who wanted Australian football to be his gift to China.

I travelled to China 14 times in 2016. The pursuit of further commercial opportunities, a more expansive program of activities (which included the goal of building a school footy program), and planning for the game we wanted to play the following year, required significant time on the ground. KT was on several of these trips, and with Promise we explored the China opportunity together. The travel pattern became very familiar. Relationships with Cathay Pacific, which would soon become an important partner of the club, and the Portman Ritz Carlton, run by avid Port Adelaide fan Robert Blackborough, were very important.

Together, we looked at potential venues for the match, including Shanghai Stadium, as well as the venue used for the 2010 exhibition game between Melbourne and Brisbane. When KT and I first arrived at Jiangwan Stadium, it was being used as a driving range. Golf balls were scattered across the untended, inconsistently grassed surface. This initial memory of Jiangwan was still vivid when, little more than a year later, our players described it as the best surface they had ever played on.

We someone managed to capture the attention of the local government, largely thanks to the support of our Consulate General in Shanghai. These were new experiences, in formal settings, but I believe we gave a good account of ourselves. Australians tend to communicate in a direct manner; as Paul Keating once suggested, we pride ourselves on speaking frankly, a style which is not always appreciated or appropriate when dealing with other cultures in our region.

KT's style (not dissimilar to that of former South Australian premier Jay Weatherill, for whom I worked as a speechwriter and advisor for international engagement, and with whom I will work again at Minderoo Foundation) was perfectly suited to high-level conversations in China. He was humble, understated, and used language that emphasised mutual benefit and long-term partnership. As a result, the relationships that were built throughout 2016 have endured.

A significant network of high-level connections was

established. We had met with Sun Weimin, the deputy head of the Shanghai Municipal Government Sports Bureau. He was both charming and supportive. A strong relationship had been established with the Yangpu District Government, the district in which Jiangwan Stadium was located, and with the Jiangwan Stadium itself. We had introduced ourselves to JUSS Events, the state-owned events company that ran the Shanghai Masters tennis, the Formula One Grand Prix, and the Diamond League athletics meet. They ultimately managed the organisation of the match. The time spent developing these relationships was not wasted.

Port Adelaide lost convincingly to Sydney by 67 points on a miserable day in Sydney in early August 2016 (definitively and mathematically putting an end to our finals aspirations), but there was still much to do if we were to play a game in Shanghai in 2017. At Kochie's encouragement, the AFL contracted David Stevenson, who had been relieved of his position as CEO of the Western Bulldogs just prior to its ultimately successful finals campaign. This was a much-needed, and from our perspective welcomed, appointment.

Despite the Prime Minister's announcement in April, the ongoing conversations with the AFL and the fact that we had found in Gold Coast a willing opponent, it was still not certain in early October that the game would go ahead. On 17 October, David Stevenson, Promise and I travelled to China to get the final assurances the AFL required for the game to be announced by the end of the month.

At this moment, it felt very important to the broader Australian community that the vision of playing an in-season AFL match in Mainland China, was realised. The night of our arrival, I met with Tony Finocchiaro. Tony was Managing Director at Weir Group, fluent in Mandarin, with a deep understanding of Chinese government, culture and business practice. We met, and walked the streets of Shanghai, running through the possible permutations of the days that were to follow. Reflecting on this conversation at the time of writing, I cannot describe how much I miss these moments.

The first meeting the following day was with Mr Sun Weimin from the Shanghai Sports Bureau. David, Promise and I spent the hour prior to the meeting rushing from sports store to sports store in an attempt to locate a ball pump, so it was a great pleasure to present him a football, inflated, signed by the Port Adelaide team, and a letter from the Prime Minister emphasising the importance of the game to the bilateral relationship.

Mr Sun encouraged us to consider another venue, such as a university, but it was too late for us to change course so close to the announcement. He also approved of the broader Australian theme, which elevated the event as something more than sport; more a true cultural exchange. Dave was in the chair, with Promise translating, and we left the meeting thinking that we would have the approvals in place for the game to proceed. The presence of a JUSS representative, which suggested that the government would encourage their involvement, was reassuring.

Over the coming days, Dave negotiated verbal agreements with Jiangwan Stadium and a loose agreement to work with JUSS. We were able to return to Australia with the assurances needed for the game to be announced. The short, intense trip had secured the outcome that had appeared, once again, unlikely at its outset. On 26 October 2016, the chairmen and CEOs of Port Adelaide and the Gold Coast, AFL CEO Gillon McLachlan and senior executives from all parties assembled at the Chinese Museum in Melbourne to announce that the first-ever AFL game played outside Australia and New Zealand would be played at the Jiangwan Stadium in Shanghai on 14 May 2017.

The Chinese Museum was a beautifully appropriate setting for the occasion, and Gillon spoke with characteristic poise and aplomb, graciously thanking a bloke called 'Andrew Butcher' (he was referring to me) for his efforts, before Kochie spoke effusively about the game and what it meant. KT savoured the moment from behind the scenes. Were it not for their leadership, Port Adelaide would never have been part of this historic moment in the inevitable internationalisation of our extraordinary sport.

Port Adelaide's 2016 winter of discontent ended on 27 August, with a 23-point victory over the Gold Coast at Metricon Stadium in front of 9213 spectators. The next time the two sides would meet would be in front of a larger crowd, in Shanghai, on an unforgettable day in May 2017.

7 The 2016/2017 off-season

I have courage because I was born to do this.

Joan d'Arc

People often ask what we do in the off-season when working at a football club, as if inertia sets in as soon as the playing season is over. Nothing could be further from the truth, and this was particularly the case for those at Port Adelaide involved in the China project. Indeed, the months that separated the 2016 and 2017 seasons were filled with furious activity. We had a game to promote, a steep commercial imperative to satisfy – and a diplomatic opportunity to pursue.

In November 2016, several members of the executive, six players, our senior coach as well as Team China and our Aboriginal Academy side travelled to China to promote Shanghai 2017. This initiative was a considerable undertaking. Over the course of a week, hundreds of schoolchildren arrived at Century Park, Shanghai's largest park, to participate in football activities and watch the AFL-listed players train with the Aboriginal Academy. The students were participants in our nascent *Power Footy* school program, which we had started developing in August.

The idea of taking football to schools in China, as an expression of our culture and opportunity for young students to learn more about Australia, was not easy to convey. There was still no resonance of our sport in China, and highlights of Australian Rules elicited curiosity, excitement and concern in equal measure. 'Is it within the rules for one player to stand on someone's head to mark the ball?' they would ask. 'Is it safe?' But in August, Promise and I were able to convince seven or eight schools in China to get involved in the *Power Footy* program and in November we reached around 2500 students through clinics at Century Park and in the schools.

At part of this promotion, CCTV had helped arrange some ping-pong diplomacy of a different kind. Olympic champion Wang Liqin participated in a table tennis exhibition against Ken Hinkley and some of the players, as part of the promotional tour and in front of the schoolchildren attending the camp. Wang demonstrated an array of trick shots as he took on our players, who were themselves quite handy with a table tennis bat. A few of the Aboriginal Academy boys were pretty handy as well! The promotional tour was a great way to get the word out about the game.

The trip in November was also a dry run for the players and coaches, to ensure that they were comfortable with the experience of travelling to China and familiar with the surroundings when they returned for the game the following year. Coach Ken Hinkley and Chris Davies, head of the football department, travelled with six senior players: Travis Boak, Ollie Wines, Chad Wingard, Brad Ebert, Robbie Gray and Patrick Ryder.

The Portman Carlton Ritz, with Robert Blackborough paying meticulous attention to every detail, laid out the red carpet, and there were few issues. The players appeared to thoroughly enjoy the experience. Two members of the travelling party lost their passports, which elicited a huge effort on the part of the staff at Australia's Consulate-General in Shanghai, but it was nothing compared to the disruption they would experience the following May.

CCTV covered the training camp and a documentary about Port Adelaide's push into the Middle Kingdom appeared on Chinese television on Christmas Eve. A press conference was also held at the hotel on the final morning, with KT speaking as well as the deputy head of Shanghai's Sports Bureau, Sun Weimin, the mayor of Yangpu, and Australian consul-general to Shanghai, Graeme Meehan. The event attracted around 40 journalists from a variety of agencies. These early efforts to spread the message of Australian football was important.

In early December, we signed a partnership agreement with Cathay Pacific. It was the product of a relationship that had evolved over the course of the year. Cathay was a founding member of our China-focused coterie group, China Power Club, in 2016, its inaugural year. Through it, we had developed a strong relationship with its Adelaide office, led by Roz Meertens.

As we were speaking with Cathay, we were also part of a competitive process for sponsorship from China Southern Airlines. Promise and I had visited their head office in Guangzhou and spoke to executives on many occasions, and officially presented to the agent responsible for the process. We were aware that our opponents were also in the contest.

Cathay Pacific made a very strong offer, exceeding the numbers under discussion with China Southern Airlines, and we made the latter aware of this and asked for their response. We were ultimately delighted to sign with Cathay, a premium airline with which we enjoyed an excellent relationship. It ensured we stayed connected with people like Denis Way and Peter Phillips, who provided advice and support throughout the greater part of our adventure. Cathay Pacific renewed for 2018 at a higher level.

In spite of these efforts, commercial support for the game itself (as opposed to our broader *Open to the World* program) was slow in coming. Although we believed that the game in China was important because it provided the one moment in which all of our partners could come together, we struggled to articulate its deeper meaning. Our narrative lacked the seamlessness, the inevitability and assurance that it initially had when we were explaining how an involvement in an AFL club could help a Chinese company like CRED succeed in Australia. The reasoning behind the game was more complex, and our value proposition for Australian companies looking to China was initially less compelling.

The development of such a narrative can take time – but time was not on our side. The game was only announced in late October and with the Christmas holidays in Australia and Chinese New Year following in quick succession, a level of anxiety from the respective boards and commissions enveloped those responsible for meeting the commercial challenge. When a verbal agreement – and for a considerable sum – was not honoured, concern turned into scepticism and anxiety into something akin to panic. But there are always more solutions than problems, and it was important to keep the faith.

Ausgold, a mining company that had attracted considerable controversy, and its more controversial leader Sally Zou signed as the major game-day sponsor. In commercial terms, this was a significant agreement. Sally came to the club after she had seen Port Adelaide play on CCTV and was hosted at our home match against Richmond in June 2016. KT developed a strong connection with her, which helped secure this significant sponsorship in the early days of 2017. I was happy to stay well away from this one, as important as the financial support was to that first game played in China.

What became more and more clear, as we deepened our engagement in China, is that Chinese companies face much the same issues in Australia, as Australian companies in China. The reality is that the business cultures are very different, as are the political and cultural contexts. It reaffirmed our belief that Port Adelaide had a wonderful opportunity to assist Chinese businesses and business people realise their goals and dreams in Australia.

The other major agreement underpinning the revenue chase was with Tourism Australia. Led by the AFL, the partnership with Tourism Australia was predicated on the significant television audience we anticipated to achieve in China throughout the season, thanks to our partnership with CCTV. The incumbent Minister for Tourism, Steven Ciobo, was also the Member for Moncrieff on the Gold Coast and launched the partnership in February 2017 in Shanghai. These two agreements, however significant, only covered half the cost of this expensive venture.

As Port Adelaide, with some assistance from the AFL, chased our commercial imperative, we became aware of an opportunity to significantly raise the profile of our engagement in China. The prospect of a state visit in the early months of 2017 was not yet public, but we understood that a letter of invitation had been sent from the South Australian Government to Premier Li Keqiang. If he was to visit Australia, the letter suggested, he should consider taking the opportunity to come to Adelaide.

The Middle Kingdom was a strong focus for the Weatherill Government, which was served by champions of the South Australia–China relationship, such as Sean Keenihan. Former City of Adelaide Lord Mayor Alfred Huang had just finished his stint as special envoy, and the bureaucracy was well served by energetic and creative mandarins such as Ying Ying.

Some of the initiatives of the previous 12 months had seriously enhanced South Australia's engagement in China. These initiatives included a bi-lingual, English–Mandarin program at the Plympton International School, the establishment of the Chinese Consulate-General, the opening of the Bank of China, and a direct flight from Mainland China to Adelaide, which complemented the established Cathay Pacific route from Hong Kong. Would this be enough to include Adelaide on the program for Premier Li's state visit?

If Li Keqiang was to come to Adelaide, why not invite him to Alberton Oval to promote the next significant initiative in the bilateral relationship to emanate from South Australia? Over a sustained period, we put this case to everyone who would listen, including the South Australian Government and the excellent Chinese Consul-General in Adelaide, Rao Hongwei. It was ambitious, but we genuinely believed that the match in Shanghai, with the popular attention it would attract, would make a significant contribution to the diplomacy between Australia and China.

By the end of January, there was an urgent request from

the Chinese Embassy for information on our plans for 2017 – what were we planning for China and what were we about to announce. This level of interest and the urgency in the message suggested that something was up. In February 2017, I received a phone call from someone in the know. 'I have good news,' he said. 'I can't tell you what it is. But you will be very happy.' Indeed, when we found out what it was, we were ecstatic.

Pressure abounded in the early months of 2017. It became clear that participation in finals, after two disappointing seasons, was the only option. And for those who had argued for the importance of playing an official game in China, there was pressure to ensure that the game was not a financial albatross for the club. When, finally, it was announced that Premier Li Keqiang would attend our round one match against Sydney, in Sydney, and visit Port Adelaide's change rooms prior to the game, Port Adelaide's engagement with China had further credibility and the match itself an added appeal.

This certainly helped the game achieve an acceptable commercial outcome. Important commercial agreements were concluded in the days leading up to our match in Sydney on 25 March, some of which were extended and increased soon after the match. For someone committed to gradual relationship building and long-term thinking, the conversations that transpired in these early months of 2017 did not sit comfortably. But we did what was necessary to keep the fire burning.

We travelled to Canberra to discuss arrangements with the Chinese Embassy, which was understandably keen to ensure that everything went smoothly. It was further confirmation that our engagement in China was acknowledged and appreciated by both governments, probably tired by the ongoing negative sentiment which continued to shadow the relationship (and would get worse). We were told by their senior diplomats that they wanted to 'shine a light' on our engagement with China.

The day before the opening match of the season, I was asked to say a few words at Port Adelaide's Sydney Business Lunch event on Darling Harbour. It was an exciting time. When I was a kid, the days that preceded the first game of footy were the most exciting; the weeks preceding it filled with cricket. The evolution of international cricket meant the domestic summer finished earlier, leaving a vacuum in which to dream about what the upcoming football season could bring. Where once this period separated cricket from football, it now seemed to separate nothing from everything.

It felt as though we were either on the precipice, or on the cusp. It had felt like that for a long time, and it was not just those engaged in the China project who felt this to be true. The playing group, coaches and CEO no doubt shared these sentiments. At the end of the speech, I asserted that when 'our boys take the four points tomorrow – with the Prime Minister and Premier Li looking on – and in the embrace of a country of over one billion people, the nation will see that we are on the cusp of an extraordinary moment'. The words 'take the four points' elicited a ripple of laughter across the room. At a Port Adelaide function. Within the bosom of a club that for 147 years had demanded success, there were people who laughed at the assertion that we would win.

Maybe we were closer to the precipice than we cared to admit?

8 Sports diplomacy

A ball bounced … and the whole world was shocked. The big globe was set in motion by a tiny globe.

Zhou Enlai

Port Adelaide's engagement in China, and its contribution to the bilateral relationship, must be considered in the broader political and geopolitical contexts. When Trump was elected President of the United States, a Chinese official was quoted asserting that the chances of war between the US and China was growing, and China was preparing for a potential military confrontation. China was tightening controls on external investment flows and looking to eliminate frivolous investment in sports clubs; in Australia there was a growing suspicion of investment emanating from China and of Chinese influence on our democratic and learning institutions.

These developments complicated a relationship that, from the Australian perspective, was in any case largely for its economic potential. There was an emotional distance between Australia and China, and in that vacant space emerged an opportunity to use sport to bring our two peoples closer. Safe ground is needed on which we can come together and reset the parameters of the relationship.

Port Adelaide spoke of sports diplomacy a lot. It is an abused and misunderstood term. I wrote my Masters' thesis (supervised by China expert Gerry Groot and Nick Jose, former Cultural Attaché in our Embassy in Beijing) on public diplomacy between Australia and China, so I am familiar with the field. It was frustrating to see others further confusing the concept.

On a technical level, sports diplomacy is considered a form of public diplomacy, which aims to communicate and promote a positive impression of one country to the people of other countries. Any form of diplomacy suggests an involvement of sovereign governments. Sports diplomacy is more than bringing together a few people from different countries to watch a game of sport. From our experience, however, the purest form of sports diplomacy is one born of genuine people-to-people exchange, and the most important form of sports diplomacy is one that emphasises mutual understanding through sport.

In the past, sports diplomacy has been most famous for its contribution to diplomatic breakthroughs between estranged countries. Sport has contributed to political rapprochement between the United States and China ('ping-pong diplomacy' in 1971), and between Cuba and the United States ('baseball diplomacy' in 1999, and again in 2015).

China deployed sports diplomacy to deepen relationships between ideological stablemates in the early years of the People's Republic (from 1949, China used sport to develop friendly relationship with other countries in the Communist bloc). Australia and China, however, are not ideologically aligned. Nor are we searching for a diplomatic breakthrough; Gough Whitlam had achieved normalisation in 1972.

Sports that are commonly enjoyed by both countries, such

as basketball and soccer, relate to national prestige and are therefore played on dangerous terrain. The 1972 hockey series between Canada and USSR was ultimately considered an example of positive sports diplomacy but could easily have been derailed by several ugly incidents. Although the series was designed to achieve friendship through hockey, a Canadian player made a throat-slitting gesture to his opponent while another, on instructions from his assistant coach, intentionally broke the ankle of his Soviet opponent.

Countries with formal sports diplomacy policies, such as Australia and France, often focus on initiatives designed to achieve an economic outcome. There is value in this, but what is most needed between Australia and China is an unthreatening platform on which to develop greater understanding. If greater intercultural understanding in domestic audiences makes for a more enabling environment for effective diplomacy, the choice of sport is important.

Contests involving sports that appeal to national prestige could easily have adverse diplomatic consequences. Australian Football offers little to China in the form of national prestige, the outcome of the game is irrelevant. It could, however, help develop a positive narrative between the two countries and their leaders, and pique the popular interest in Australia, where understanding of China remains superficial.

Turnbull was the first to grasp this opportunity, followed by Premier Li Keqiang in 2017. And it became part of the story of their personal relationship, when Premier Li mentioned in their bilateral meeting at the sidelines of APEC in November 2017 that he had a picture of them wearing footy scarfs in his office in Beijing.

When surveyed, Port Adelaide members consistently showed that our engagement piqued their interest in Chinese history and culture, and the 6000 Australians who ultimately travelled to Shanghai to watch the first AFL match to be played in China would have returned with a completely different understanding of that country.

Sports diplomacy shouldn't be considered useful when estranged countries seek rapprochement, but as an ongoing opportunity to develop greater understanding between the peoples. Popular understanding enables effective foreign policy.

It should not be assumed that understanding leads to affection – it can sometimes lead to contempt – but foreign policy is stronger when it responds to an informed popular opinion; one that is less susceptible to the dog whistle of ignorance, fear or xenophobia. And we were confident that our supporters would enjoy their interaction with the Chinese people as much as we did.

At this moment, however, we were swimming into a powerful wave that drew its energy from increasing geostrategic competition, an increasingly assertive China, and populist domestic politics within Australia. Nonetheless, over the five years of our strategy, Port Adelaide contributed what it could to sports diplomacy between Australia and China, and there was no more exciting day than 25 March 2017.

9 The day that changed everything

Two worlds collided
And they could never tear us apart
from 'Never Tear Us Apart' by INXS

When the coach and players returned to the change room following their 28-point victory over Sydney on 25 March 2017, Port Adelaide's season suddenly appeared to be on a different trajectory than it had just a few hours earlier. Both joy and relief were palpable. After spending the long months of the off-season on the precipice, it felt as though the character of the season had been transformed. However, the day itself had been highly stressful for those involved.

Two days earlier, KT and I had been invited to the Official Reception of Premier Li and Madame Cheng in the Great Hall at Parliament House in Canberra. A formal state affair, my table was directly adjacent to the head table. For a footy club to have a seat at the table was already exceptional. Each of the official speeches referred to Shanghai2017, and to the fact that Li and Turnbull would attend the match in Sydney. Turnbull spoke first and described sport as fertile soil for our friendship to grow, followed by Leader of the Opposition Bill Shorten, who took a little longer to reflect on the significance. Premier Li then spoke at some length on the significance of an Australian football game that would soon be played in China.

I appreciated Premier Li's style. He spoke without prepared notes, relaxed at the lectern with one foot often hooked behind the other. Moments of levity were injected into a speech that included serious commentary on the state of the bilateral relationship. He compared the relationship China had with Australia to flying through a lightning storm, and noted that China pursues an independent foreign policy, perhaps in contrast to Australia's deference to the United States. But he was a natural diplomat, delivering subtle and not-so-subtle messages in a calm, succinct and agreeable manner.

A moment of levity in a speech – like seeing a game of footy during a state visit – provide opportunities for momentary respite in a relationship that is likely to experience turbulence as the balance of power changes in the region we share. This is why Port Adelaide's efforts to engage with China, although designed to achieve a commercial imperative, are far more than that. When our national anthem played in the Great Hall that day, I was deeply moved. The walk across the bridge over Lake Burley Griffin back to Civic was an opportunity for a pleasant moment of reflection, before the seemingly endless fury of our work began anew.

As we focused on our big event two days later, an event transpired, I have been reliably informed, within the confines of Parliament House that would affect the Turnbull Government's relationship with China. According to this account, the Australian Government had, prior to Li's arrival, agreed that Turnbull and Li would sign an MoU during the state visit, regarding its participation in the Belt and Road Initiative. Following the lunch held in the Premier's honour at Parliament House on 23 March, a meeting took place between

Turnbull and Barnaby Joyce, then leader of the National Party and Deputy Prime Minister. The full Cabinet was not present, according to this account, but a tense discussion ensued, during which it was decided Australia would ask to remove this signing and announcement from the program.

Australia would have been the first Western country to agree to participate in BRI. At the time of writing, BRI remains a divisive issue in Australia, with Victoria a target for those who see it as antithetical to the national interest. It remains interesting, in retrospect, to consider the apparent incoherence within government at the time. If the account was accurate, the government's reversal would have caused the Chinese Premier embarrassment. This alleged incident was never made public and, on the surface, the bilateral still appeared to be in reasonable shape at the time. But by the end of the year, it had deteriorated substantially. And further deterioration would follow.

We travelled on to Sydney, participated in Port Adelaide's Sydney Business Lunch on Friday and prepared as best we could for Saturday. A lot could go wrong, and much was out of our control with arrangements between the Department of Prime Minister and Cabinet, the AFL and the SCG Trust. It was vital that the change room visit go smoothly, and not interfere with the preparation for the game – other than the professional respect for the footy department and acknowledgement that they would also be nervous and excited about the challenge before them. It was a massive day for the whole club, with so much at stake.

As we waited in the hotel lobby prior to departure, one of our guests, a successful businessman from China, arrived dressed as Mao Zedong. Beyond his business interests, this gentleman had a sideline acting in historical documentary-movies. Why he came dressed this way, I'll never know – but from the outset, I knew it would be a problem. This was communicated to his minder, who tried to convince me that it wouldn't be an issue. It would be, I retorted. And it was.

We took a bus together to the SCG and after quickly inspecting the SCG Trust Suite, where high-profile personalities are entertained on game day, we assembled in the Port Adelaide change rooms. It was a nervous wait. We are abundantly aware that AFL rules stipulate you cannot use mobile phones in the change rooms prior to games, to limit the potential for insider information being used for gambling. But this was lost on Sally Zou, who used her phone liberally to take photos in the change rooms. This before the eyes of the AFL's integrity officers, whose rebuke and subsequent fine we (deservedly) copped.

From the moment the entourage entered the room, any sense of planning or schedule was soon forgotten. We understood that a large delegation would be present, as five ministers and three vice-ministers were travelling with Premier Li – but we were not prepared for the size and energy of the entourage that would burst through the room five minutes earlier than planned.

Our group included KT, Promise, Chen and a few important supporters of our *Open to the World* campaign (Gui, Sally Zou, Nicho Teng and his associate Wang Kaitang). I stepped back and observed proceedings from a safe distance. Any semblance of order and planning that we believed was in place immediately disappeared.

Premier Li's entourage, and staff from both the Prime Minister's Office and the Department of Prime Minister and

Cabinet were accompanied by a large media pack. The group numbered several score. Kochie immediately took control of proceedings. Turnbull was wearing his Sydney Swans scarf and, as agreed prior by PM&C and the Chinese Embassy, Kochie threw a Port Adelaide scarf over Premier Li. He walked the line of Port Adelaide's party until he reached KT, whose natural disposition took over.

The photo of the ensuing warm embrace of two complete strangers – one, a seasoned statesman and the other the face of an ambitious sports diplomacy initiative – tells the story of Port Adelaide's engagement in China.

Premier Li then spoke to footballer Chen, remarked on the size of his biceps, and was invited to handball the ball to the PM. This was not according to script but Kochie was unconcerned about such trivialities at this point, so instead of Li handballing to Chen who would then hand the ball to Turnbull, the ball was handballed in a proficient manner directly to the PM who, thankfully, successfully grasped the ball. The gesture was then returned to Premier Li who *did* drop the ball but didn't seem overly fussed.

The PM's minders were keen for the potentially embarrassing episode to end so as quickly as the mob had arrived, they left the Port Adelaide change rooms and made for the SCG Trust Suite upstairs. Ken had not even finished addressing the players, so didn't have the chance to speak to Premier Li as was planned, but I don't suppose he was overly fussed either.

At the official welcome function upstairs, we were soon made aware of an earlier incident. The businessman who had come dressed as an historic figure had predictably not been allowed into the room. Our head of commercial, Damien

McDowell, had scrambled to get him in different attire so that he did not miss the event entirely. The show rolled on. Li, Turnbull, AFL Chairman Michael Fitzpatrick and Kochie were each soon due to give short speeches but before official proceedings began, PM and Premier went to the balcony to look over the field – at which point some wag from the crowd threw Li a Sydney Swans scarf. This improvisation was most unwelcome! Looking back on some of the photos taken of the moment, it appears Kochie tried to remove the Swans scarf from Li's shoulders, but around his shoulders it stayed – much to the chagrin of every Port Adelaide person present!

Back inside the SCG Trust Suite, the formalities started. We had been told in the pre-event briefings that our Chairman could not talk for longer than four minutes, including translation, a task to which he stuck admirably. The same instruction was clearly not conveyed to the AFL Chairman, who spoke for an eternity. By the time the national leaders were due to speak, it was already precariously close to game time. They were aware of the timing and no doubt cut their speeches short, Premier Li using the two scarfs around his neck to make a point about China's policy of neutrality and non-interference in the domestic affairs of a sovereign state. It was an example of the sublime art of diplomacy – no opportunity is wasted to subtly but favourably shift thinking.

In his classic book *The First Resort of Kings,* Richard Arndt describes gift-giving as the 'diplomat's opening'. We had always aimed to give meaningful gifts to demonstrate our desire to build relationships on trust and understanding. As part of David's speech, he invited Gavin Wanganeen to the stage to give Premier Li a Port Adelaide jumper decorated with a painting of sampan fishing vessels. There was an interesting back-story to this gift. Former Chinese President Hu Jintao believed that rock paintings in Amurdak country, not far from the eastern shallows of Van Diemen Gulf in northern Australia, prove that Ming dynasty expeditionary fleets reached Australian shores in the 1420s.

This history is disputed, but Gavin's brilliant depiction, which featured both a dragon and a serpent emerging from the vessel, clearly pleased the Chinese leader.

A gift of a book was also presented for Li's wife, Madame Cheng Hong, a professor who specialises in naturalism in American literature. Premier Li reciprocated by presenting a large plate with a picture of an English-style sailing vessel to Kochie, perhaps as an acknowledgement of the club's origins in Adelaide's port, or to directly link the two gifts (we had informed the appropriate officials of our gift a week earlier).

Outside seats were allocated only for VIPs so there was a scramble for seats. Many of the guests were intent on photos with Li, others with the PM, and they surrounded them like moths to a flame. The scene was chaotic but settled down by the first bounce. Chen was perched in the row behind Li, explaining the game to him in Mandarin. Next to Chen was Zhang Lu, the rock-star translator to China's prominent political figures. As Li and Turnbull settled into the game, Port Adelaide started strongly in an even first quarter, and was behind by one point at the first change against last year's grand finalists.

The leaders left the SCG, Port Adelaide prevailed, and we fixed our focus firmly on making the first AFL match to be played in China a day to remember.

10 Game week, Shanghai 2017

Fatigue makes cowards of us all.

Vince Lombardi, NFL coach and player

For those at Port Adelaide involved in the organisation of the game in Shanghai, the lead-up through April and May was exciting but exhausting. Working over weekends became the norm, as Port Adelaide and the AFL faced the incredible complexity of arranging an official AFL match in China. As well as the match itself, events were planned throughout the game week and to facilitate this a member of our events team, Bec Quartermaine, was based in Shanghai for over a month prior to the game. We arrived in Shanghai with equal measures of excitement and fatigue.

The game was played in round eight (a lucky number in China), and Port Adelaide's season was delicately poised. Following convincing victories against Carlton (90 points) and Brisbane (83 points), we went down to West Coast by 10 points at home, despite having five more scoring shots. The match in Shanghai was looming as pivotal to our season. Early in the game week, some were describing the game being played in China as a distraction.

Outside Adelaide, the football media hadn't shown a lot of interest until the week of the game. Interestingly, the attitude of the articles in the Australian press changed over the course of the week from cynicism to praise. Gold Coast Suns coach Rodney Eade set the tone before his team left Australia, complaining that 'you can't get a direct flight ... by the time we get there it will be about 20 hours, 21 hours'. The opposition coach also expressed concerns about the pollution, announcing that 'we won't take any players who have asthma or some respiratory problems anyway'. A photographer from the *Age* picked up the theme and used a yellow filter in a photo to make the air appear more polluted than it actually was. Past champions adopted a similarly cynical approach. Premiership player Tim Watson said that an 'overseas trip mid-season has the capacity to derail' the seasons of the two teams involved, while premiership coach Paul Roos labelled the exercise 'ridiculous'.

Already in China, we were aware of these disappointing but perhaps not surprising comments. Australian football has a narrow experience, with little exposure to the norms of international sport. Those who had such experience quickly moved to ridicule commentary that described the experience as unduly arduous. It was pointed out that A-League soccer teams often travel further to compete in the Asian Champions League, and Australia's Super Rugby teams often travel to South Africa to compete. One commentator noted that Shanghai was hardly a 'backwater' and suggested the game would help the AFL 'broaden its horizons and toughen up a little'.

Our footy department didn't buy into this recalcitrant narrative, even though the game was played at a crucial juncture of the season for the team. The club was ready to make history. We were well looked after by Cathay Pacific and travelled in comfort. The players loved staying at the Portman Ritz Carlton and appreciated the Port Adelaide connection. Hotel manager Robert Blackborough's father had worked at the Alberton Hotel back in the day.

The players seemed happy to be in Shanghai, and it was great to see them there. AFL offers many opportunities and perks for those good enough to make it – but one thing our sport does not yet offer is the opportunity to perform internationally. Hopefully, we have taken a step to remedy that. The players were positive about the experience when talking to the media. Jack Hombsch said the 'media exaggerated a lot of the conditions'; Brad Ebert lauded the experience as a 'resounding success'. They had open minds and appreciated the chance to be part of a unique moment for our game.

This belied the significant struggle in the preceding week to ensure that the game ran smoothly. As is often the case in China, it is important to understand the political context. Sunday 14 May 2017 was the opening day of a two-day Belt and Road Initiative (BRI) Summit being held in Beijing, which was attended by 29 heads of state. Within the People's Republic of China, this was considered an auspicious event. President Xi claimed that BRI, a modern version of the ancient network of trade routes known collectively as the Silk Road, would be the beginning of a new Golden Age of globalisation. Xi proclaimed in support of BRI that history 'shows that civilisation thrives with openness and that nations prosper from exchange'. Others argued that BRI was a play for geostrategic dominance. Whatever the case, nothing would be allowed to divert attention away from it.

There were also issues specific to Shanghai. Han Zheng, the Communist Party Secretary of Shanghai, was rumoured to be up for promotion and was keen to ensure that no last-minute events would impact his rise. This confluence of political considerations was such that risk aversion was the only priority for local authorities, which no doubt looked upon the prospect of 6000 travelling Australian football supporters with disquiet.

Challenges, there were many. We were informed upon arrival that there would be no alcohol available at the ground, and a requirement for a minimum police presence of several hundred (for which we would be obliged to financially compensate). The Taste of Australia festival – stalls serving Australian food and wine in the precinct just outside the game – was to be reduced, hemmed in by a fence, and devoid of alcohol. There would no access for supporters to the planned open training session the day before the game.

The overwhelming sentiment in the Port Adelaide camp was that the experience of Port Adelaide people, who had spent good money to travel halfway around the world to support their team, would be diminished by these changes. In retrospect, we perhaps undersold the Port Adelaide supporters' understanding of the significance of this day. They understood and, I think, were proud that they were part of an historic moment – and an absence of alcohol on game day was not going to diminish or trivialise what the Port Adelaide supporters were experiencing together.

Dave Stevenson, now the project lead, worked closely with JUSS Events Company. Once we had introduced the organisation to the AFL, they remained the focal point of the relationship. We believed that JUSS, a state-owned organisation that ran the Formula One, Masters and various other international sporting events in China, was best placed to navigate the complex government system. Under extremely difficult and tense circumstances, Dave, with JUSS, negotiated a range of concessions. The 'open' training remained closed to supporters, as we had not applied for the appropriate permit, but there would be alcohol served in hospitality tents at the game. As tickets to the premium hospitality areas went for as much as $600, it was a relief that there would be alcohol available! Taste of Australia would go ahead, but in a diminished form with alcohol 'sampling' only.

As Dave was addressing these issues, we were also seeking to confirm the broadcast of the game on CCTV. This relationship had broken down following the first match of the season, for reasons that remain largely beyond our understanding (although I strongly suspect we had been caught cheekily trying to integrate an advertisement for Tourism Australia into the broadcast), but we desperately wanted the national broadcaster to cover this historic match. This conversation was weeks old and it seemed that it would come down to the wire.

The Australian diplomatic corps, both from the Embassy in Beijing and the Consulate-General in Shanghai, were brilliant. Generous, patient, tireless, professional. We had great support from Ambassador Jan Adams, as well as Consul-General Meehan, and there were those at the coalface who contributed incredible energy to the cause and believed in its merit. Lisa Bateman, from the Australian Embassy in Beijing, had led discussions with CCTV during this period and, to our great relief, we were informed two days before the game that the game would be indeed shown live on the national broadcaster.

There were myriad other issues needing to be addressed, the natural product of a moment in which thousands of Australians would descend on Shanghai. Time and time again, we turned to our diplomats. A journalist, missing the correct documentation and unable to pay the required deposit, had his camera confiscated at the Shanghai airport. Bonnie Hoffman from the Consulate-General worked with her counterparts in the Shanghainese Municipal Government to resolve the situation. It happened early in the week, but some deft diplomacy ensured the situation was not repeated. Australia is incredibly well served by our professional diplomats.

Every issue provided an opportunity to see how government works in China. On Wednesday morning, Deputy Consul-General Marcus Longham and Bonnie represented our concerns to the local government authorities. Dave and I were in the meeting, which followed standard diplomatic procedures, one side sitting along a long table facing their counterparts. On the Chinese side, the deputy mayor of Yangpu (the district in which the game would be played) was present, as was the chief of Yangpu police.

The deputy mayor, supportive of the game when we had frequently dealt with him in the past, appeared to defer to his chief of police. Though the Chinese system is hierarchical, it is also famous for 'stove-piping'. This happens when individual ministries and other hierarchies share information up and down the chain of command but not horizontally. The chief of police remained on script and was unmoved in the face of Marcus's representations and our arguments. No concessions were made.

The meeting the following afternoon at the Shanghai Public Security Bureau (PSB) headquarters, at which one representative each from JUSS, the AFL and Port Adelaide was present, was even more interesting. As most of the travelling fans were there to support Port Adelaide, I was asked by the Police Bureau whether Port Adelaide supporters were of good character, and whether there was a history of violence between the supporters of Port Adelaide and Gold Coast! I had to pause for a moment to keep a straight face before I explained that there were seldom, if ever, violent incidents at Australian football grounds and the rivalry we had with the Gold Coast was too young to elicit tension let alone violence. You'd more likely see the chairmen of the respective clubs come to blows than the supporters!

The PSB may have assumed that Australian football supporters would be similar to soccer fans in China, who see themselves as representing fashionable counterculture, unconstrained by the mores of society. Supporters of Australian Rules football, if anything, reflect positive aspects of Australian culture. Certainly, in Shanghai, they were open-minded, vibrant, and inclusive – Australia at its best.

On Friday, Promise and I had to travel by bullet train to Ji'nan, in Shandong Province, where a working group session between the South Australian Government and its counterparts from Shandong, with whom SA has a sister-state relationship, was taking place. There, Port Adelaide signed a memorandum of understanding with the Shandong Sports Bureau, and universities from both provinces, on sports science. We have believed for some time that sports science offers a great potential as a service export to China. The event went smoothly, and the train journey offered an opportunity to gather our thoughts.

On Friday, the events schedule was well underway with a cocktail party held at the Portman Carlton Ritz. The big event was held the following night: a $600 per head gala dinner, at which political, business and sporting figures were in attendance. Premier Weatherill made a great speech and witnessed the extension of our agreement with MJK International Holdings Ltd. (This was a big deal, but within a year, its chairman was under investigation in China, and the relationship was severed.) The program for the evening was crowded and not everything went perfectly to plan, but there was an incredible vibe in the room.

With a lived, rather than pre-conceived, experience of China, and Shanghai in particular, the Australian media were now far more positive. Some experienced football journalists likened the build-up to the game with that of a grand final. The vibe wasn't the only noticeable element on the night of the gala dinner – there was also a lot of money in that room! There were premiers, ministers, billionaires and one player of the century, Leigh Matthews. Not a bad gathering for an event, which had been for so long the subject of ridicule and ignorance.

Doing something of such an unprecedented nature, with relatively limited resources, is not easy but perhaps we suffered from the fundamental mistake of trying to replicate an Australian experience in China. We wanted the travelling supporters' experience to resemble their experience at Adelaide Oval – but this ignores the need for an intercultural mind and defeats the purpose of holding a game in China. You can't appropriate the Australian experience and replicate it in a Chinese context. Even the gala dinner, which started at a time we would consider appropriate in Australia, was far later than was usual in China. But everyone appeared happy and ready for the big event, now imminent.

The week, while both tense and exhausting, had some nice moments. On Saturday, a small press conference for the South Australian media was held at the top of the Peace Hotel. It aimed to promote the memorandum of understanding, signed a day earlier in Ji'nan. I enjoyed standing there with Jay, my former boss, and my current boss KT, as two streams of my career merged. On Wednesday morning Promise and I also paid a quick visit to Gui. It was only 20 months since I had first met him, and much had been achieved in that time. He offered the wise advice that the work had been done and the rest was largely out of my control, so it was important to enjoy the moment and 'let it flow'.

But generally, the week had been tough. As gameday approached, the nights were longer. Four hours sleep had turned into three and then into two. When I woke up on Sunday morning, I was tired but happy that Port Adelaide was on the cusp of an extraordinary moment, and those who had the vision, leadership and energy to make it happen would be there to enjoy the moment together. Vincent van Gogh once wrote that 'great things are done by a series of small things brought together'. The accumulation of effort and risk-taking over many hours had given Port Adelaide the chance to be a part of the first official AFL match to be played in China.

11 The game, 14 May 2017

What would life be if we had no courage to attempt anything?

Vincent Van Gogh

In 2017, Mother's Day fell on 12 May. Luckily for me, Mum had travelled to Shanghai to see the game, so I didn't have to go far to wish her happy Mother's Day. With sleep deprivation now a constant companion, I woke early and followed the same routine as every other day I stayed at the Portman: a (very) slow jog down Nanjing Road West, followed by a (very) short session in the gym, followed by an omelette. Mum and Sally joined me for breakfast, a welcome distraction.

Port Adelaide staff met early to go over the final details. Sally had helped me prepare messages for the China team at Port Adelaide (which now counted seven); people who had worked their guts out over the past months to make the game possible. The China Engagement team, who made this game happen, consisted of Xu Nuo, Claire Bunten, Shane Smith, Damien McDowell, Adam Thomson, and Li Jinsong. We shared a glass of champagne to celebrate, then began the last leg of what had been a long march, each of us going our different ways.

Promise and I travelled to Jiangwan Stadium, arriving at 10.30 am. The weather was extraordinary, the traffic accommodating. Many Port Adelaide supporters were already there, soaking in the atmosphere, the vibe happy and positive; people were on holiday, absorbing new sights, sounds and smells among a familiar sea of black, white, and teal.

My first task was to greet Jay, who pressed the flesh. We made our way to the Taste of Australia Festival. Although the final product was very different to what we had envisaged, it served a purpose and gave supporters something to do before the game. Catherine Sayers from Food SA had done an excellent job in very difficult circumstances. Peter Goers from the ABC was there, clearly enjoying himself, and I stole another quick moment with Sal and Mum.

My day was spent in the President's Stand, where government officials congregated. It was not perfect; there were problems, for example, with car access for senior Australian officials, but to their credit there were few complaints. The mayor of Yangpu, Mr Xie Jiangang, arrived first and remembered me from the press conference the previous November. The assistant minister of the central government's Sports Bureau, Li Yingchuan, was next, followed by Keith Pitt, then Australia's assistant minister for trade, tourism, and investment, as well as the ministers for trade from both South Australia and Victoria. Weng Tiehui, vice-mayor, Shanghai Municipal Government, arrived wearing a teal-coloured top – just one of many senior Chinese leaders who attended Port Adelaide events and matches wearing teal-coloured ties and clothing.

The crowd was building nicely, the atmosphere a cross between the grand final and a festival. KT was asked to address the players and coaches before the game, a nice touch given his personal commitment and advocacy for the project.

The enigmatic John Butcher defies Gui's prediction and goals versus Fremantle, September 2015.

AFL CEO Gillon McLachlan, Prime Minister Malcolm Turnbull, Shanghai CRED Chairman Gui Guojie, and PAFC CEO Keith Thomas at the announcement: 14 April 2016.

Ollie Wines and Brad Ebert mixing with their new fans.
Promotional Tour 2016.

Ollie and Chad take on China's Olympic Champion, Wang Liqin.
Promotional Tour 2016.

Gavin Wanganeen presents a gift to Premier Li Keqiang, 25 March 2017.

KT, SA Premier Jay Weatherill and the author speak to the media on the Bund, the day before PAFC's historic first match in China, 2017.

PAFC putting a flag in the ground, Shanghai, 2017.

The extraordinary Robbie Gray on the attack versus Gold Coast in Shanghai, 2017.

Fans swelling with pride at what the club had achieved: an in-season match in China, 2017.

PAFC was proud to partner with The University of Adelaide from 2018, to provide a better experience for international students. Alumnus Tom Jonas helps KT and former Executive Dean of the Faculty of the Professions, Christopher Findlay, launch the partnership.

Ollie Wines takes on Geelong at Adelaide Oval, 22 June 2019. Scott Lycett looks on.

Flashpoint! Steven Motlop about to kick the winning goal in Showdown 44, 2018.

Captain Tom Jonas up against Melbourne's Sam Weideman at the MCG, Round 1, 23 March 2019.

I doubt that professional athletes need extra inspiration before entering the contest, and I suspect our players knew that the day was important to the club, but it was nonetheless appreciated. They were exceptionally accommodating and supportive throughout the project.

In the President's Stand, there were meeting rooms that belied the tired general appearance of the stadium. China does ceremony well. The room was prepared for a formal meeting, but the formalities were relaxed (or ignored). This was possible only because of the incredibly positive atmosphere that had enveloped the event. As premier of South Australia, Jay was the highest-ranking Australian Government official under the official order of precedence, and began speaking with the mayor of Yangpu, before he was usurped by the central government minister. The scene was chaotic, people swapped seats and others mingled, trying to get involved in sub-meetings within meetings.

Chairman David Koch presented gifts to the central government's Administration of Sports and to the mayor of Yangpu, and was given reciprocal gifts, and Gold Coast chairman Tony Cochrane presented two Gold Coast jumpers. Jay presented Vice-Mayor Weng with a gift on our behalf: a jumper with a similar design to the one painted by Gavin Wanganeen for Premier Li, but this time with a magnolia flower in the middle to signify the important role that Shanghai had played. The jumper was presented in a gift box with a note from Port Adelaide Football Club.

Everyone then made their way from the belly of the stand to their seats in time for the national anthems; government officials seated at tables in the front row, everyone else sitting behind. Team China was on the field, singing 'March of the Volunteers' with such gusto that it could be heard around the ground. When it came time for 'Advance Australia Fair', the first bars of Port Adelaide's club song were accidentally played over the loudspeaker. I was sitting next to Lisa Bateman, who uttered, 'Oh, no,' (or words to that effect) when she realised what was happening. The error was soon corrected. It lasted long enough to be funny, but not so long as to become a diplomatic incident. And our fans loved it!

Sitting in a President's Stand full of government officials, I perhaps had the easiest role of the day. The DFAT officials and their counterparts from the Chinese Government ensured that nothing went awry. I was able to take in the day, allowing the moments to soak into the memory, where they will stay. This was particularly the case after Port Adelaide had established their command of the game during the second quarter. For all the challenges and complexity, we had experienced and overcome, the implementation of the event itself was without hiccup.

The game experience was the sum of several stand-out moments. The playing of the national anthems was one such moment. The fans' anthem, INXS classic 'Never Tear Us Apart' sung with passion on a warm spring day in Shanghai, was another. Justin Westhoff kicked a freakish soccer goal from the sideline, and the sublime Robbie Gray displayed habitual brilliance. Port Adelaide's control of the middle two quarters of the game was absolute, to the point that the officials around me suggested diplomatically that the spectacle would be enhanced if the game were closer. Though I responded with an agreeable smile, the comfortable margin allowed some selfish moments soaking in the beauty of what was unfolding, on the field and in the stands.

The event represented the best of Australia. Local authorities had feared that opposing groups of inebriated Australian fans could only produce friction or violence, but Port Adelaide fans who travelled to Shanghai, and other Australians who had made their way via temporary residences around Asia, turned out to be exemplary ambassadors. Their celebration was passionate and friendly, and I felt proud to be among them. By the end of the game the local police also became engaged as spectators. Jack Hombsch noted to the Australian media that 'some of the police officers were getting involved towards the end! Hopefully we've picked up some new fans. As Port Adelaide staff left the ground after the game, there were surreal images of local police officers wearing PAFC scarves as they cycled home, smiling and laughing. The experience was certainly not what they had been expecting a few days earlier, when their leaders were trying to gauge the likelihood of opposing fans resorting to violence!

Following the game and the presentation of trophies and medals (a little over the top perhaps for a minor round fixture, notwithstanding the game's historic status), and after I had seen the government officials to their respective cars, I made my way to Sally and Mum in the outer. These were my favourite moments of the day: seeing the pride and joy on the face of all Port Adelaide people – fans, players, staff – who had experienced the day together.

The experience, if not the contest, was reviewed favourably. Although the Australian media showed little interest leading into the week of the game, between Monday 8 May and the following Tuesday, 65 articles about the game appeared in the mainstream Australian press, and 126 across Chinese and other international media platforms including the UK's *Daily Star* and BBC, and US-based global cable and satellite sports TV channel ESPN. In the aftermath of the game, the response from the media was overwhelmingly positive. A lived experience of China had a massive, positive influence on the media's perception, the build-up had compared with that of a grand final. The project was judged a success.

Exhaustion and relief led to an early night, but there was ample time to reflect on what had just happened when Sally and I spent two weeks travelling through Finland and Russia after the game. While with friends on the island off Tampere, two hours' drive from Helsinki, I took a break from the pleasurable routine of saunas and reading to listen to the call of our game against Geelong at Skilled Stadium (the internet can be a wonderful thing!). We fell just short, in controversial circumstances, in a game that in retrospect typified the whole season.

12 Interlude: Port Adelaide in China, through the eyes of Ian Wilson, head of the Port Adelaide Football Club cheer squad

How long have I supported Port Adelaide, you ask? As long as I have been alive. I have been involved on a regular basis since 1966, when the first Port Adelaide cheer squad was officially formed. My brother John was an official member of the first-ever cheer squad and I tagged along.

If someone had asked me back then if Port Adelaide would ever play a game in China, I would have said, no way! Not even in 1997 when they entered the AFL would I have dreamt they would play a game there. Nor ten years ago. No one could have envisaged this happening.

But when Port Adelaide first announced it wanted to do something in China, I thought it a good idea to look outside Australia and expand the AFL into other countries. A lot of people expected us to fall on our faces, but they were wrong. The direction the club took was the right one. It was courageous leadership and it has worked.

Going to China showed the progress our club has made. We came into the competition, won a flag after a few years, but then had to endure all that stress from 2011. People were talking about the club going out of business. Others thought we might be relocated interstate. Playing a game in China shows everyone how much the club has achieved in the last five years.

When it was announced that we would play a match in China, I didn't know much about the place. I'm fascinated by the Terracotta Army. I had read about the sculptures when they were discovered in the 1970s and watched documentaries on them. Of course, I knew about the Great Wall – but not much, to be honest. And I knew it was a communist country and thought it would be a bit uptight. But it wasn't like that at all.

I haven't missed a game since 2011. I don't miss games. My family understands I don't miss games. My nephews know they can't have their birthday parties on game days. Once the AFL draw has been released, you arrange other important events or celebrations around it. When I hear a member of the cheer squad miss a game because of a wedding or funeral, I just think, Well, that's poor planning.

So, the weeks after it was announced that Port Adelaide would play in China, I was very stressed. People kept asking me if I would go to the game. It was expected that I would go. I was overwhelmed but eventually made the decision to go. When I finally booked my ticked, I was relieved and excited.

I was apprehensive about the trip. I didn't even have a passport! I had never been outside Australia, and if Port Adelaide hadn't played a game in China, I doubt I would have travelled overseas. Obviously, I have never gone on holiday during the season as I don't want to miss a game. And summer is my busy period at work, so it is hard to take a holiday then.

Four of us travelled to China together and we had a chance

to look around. On the drive from the airport to the city I was looking out the window thinking, Bloody hell, how big is this place. I knew Shanghai had the same population as Australia, but it is still a shock to see it for the first time.

China surprised me. Your image of any place is shaped by what you see on the news or read in the papers. China isn't always portrayed as a warm place for outsiders. But I think people are the same all over the world, and this was the case for me in China. I was struck by how friendly everyone was. The day after the game, when we were walking around the streets, we would say *ni hao* as we passed someone, and they would say it back.

But more important was that the footy team won. As soon as I arrived, I wanted to do everything I could for the club. We wanted to get everything right, so we treated it as we would any match day. Initially, the security blokes wouldn't let us on the field with our banner. But we asked someone to interpret for us and eventually we got on the field and the banner went up. That was a big relief. We didn't want to embarrass the club on international television!

I knew it was an important day for the club, so I tried to calm my emotions down and not get too carried away. I don't drink on match days, so it was interesting to see the whole cheer squad in my boat for a change. Everyone enjoyed the game as they usually did, and they probably saved a few bob because there was no alcohol available!

It was a fantastic day. When two national anthems were played before the game, it made me realise this was a unique experience. Even at the AFL grand final, there is only one national anthem played. It was a special day. When we heard the start of 'The Power To Win' played instead of the Australian national anthem, we thought our club was truly representing Australia on a special occasion, even as we realised it was a mistake. To sing 'Never Tear Us Apart' in Shanghai, feeling like we were at Adelaide Oval, was something I'll never forget. And Westhoff's goal, when he kicked it 30 metres along the ground from the boundary line, was right in front of us. Incredible.

When people ask me what China was like, I tell them without hesitating: if you get the chance to go to China, do it. China is very friendly. Sure, there is more security than we would see in Australia, but people understand that when you're in someone else's country, you need to do things their way. My personal experience of China is very different to how the country appears in the media, so if someone wants to learn about the country, they should go there. And while you're there, watch Port Adelaide play ...

Now, it seems, all Port Adelaide supporters want to go to China to see a game. They might not be able to make the major financial commitment every year, but they've seen what it is like on television, with the behind-the-scenes footage, and they're keen to go. The game and the exposure it received was a great promotion for China! We had over 5000 supporters in the first year, and around 3000 the following year.

Since I returned from China, I'm following news about China a lot more closely. I notice the bad blood between the countries, but also the positive stories. Often, the positive stories are in the business pages of the newspaper – I didn't ever read the business pages before I went to China – and often the stories are something about Port Adelaide! I noticed the other day that we were working with Penny's Hill winery to do something in China. They seem to like our wines there. I remember they were more into the reds than the whites ...

I'd love to go back. If I have the time, I'd like to travel to the Great Wall of China and see the Terracotta Army – imagine seeing them firsthand. I was very focused on the football on my first trip, but next time I return I plan to see the sights. My overriding sentiment from my trip to China was pride. I'm proud of what the club has done. It has put Port Adelaide front and centre, which is where it should be.

13 2018, Year of the Dog: A dog of a year

I conceived it, you see, but then I had to execute it. And the execution was a boring, boring affair.

Marcel Duchamp

The Beijing air was wonderfully clear in mid-January 2018. On previous trips, the smog had given the impression that we had descended upon Armageddon rather than the capital of the Middle Kingdom. But this week was different. The crispness of Beijing in the middle of winter was enough to keep you awake, without being uncomfortably cold. KT, Promise and I were back to meet with a significant State- Owned Enterprise (SOE). We had been talking to them for three years, and believed we were on the cusp of the biggest commercial deal ever done in the AFL.

The 2017 season had finished prematurely for Port Adelaide, in its elimination final with West Coast. A season of considerable promise evaporated after an immense struggle. Sitting close to the directors, the disappointment after the siren was palpable. Defeat was delivered by Luke Shuey, who kicked a goal after a siren that concluded the second half of overtime, the game having initially finished in a draw. Port Adelaide had eight more scoring shots but lost by two points.

The disappointment was all the more bitter because it appeared our fate to endure a summer in which the natural hubris of our greatest rival graduate into something far worse: actual evidence of superiority. Adelaide had endured a stellar season and was clear favourite to beat Richmond in the 2017 grand final. Alas, it was not to be. Their unexpected but emphatic defeat left our supporters swelling with schadenfreude. I didn't grasp the true meaning of schadenfreude until I started working at Port Adelaide. Port Adelaide responded to the bitter end to the season by perfectly executing its recruitment strategy in the off-season.

A sense of optimism pervaded Alberton. The world was changing in other ways, too. China was changing. Australia's relationship with China was changing. But we didn't immediately grasp the importance of these changes, and the impact it would have on our business. It was only at the beginning of 2018 that the full impact of these changes was understood and, once understood, it took time to pivot.

With concerns that China could not maintain its rate of economic growth, an incredible amount of capital was dispersed around the world. Australia was one of many countries that had benefited from this flight of capital out of China. In late 2016, however, the central government started to limit capital leaving China, which made it far more difficult to receive payments from Chinese partners. There is no point doing a deal if you can't get paid. This changed policy impacted many Australian businesses, several of which are our partners. It also impacted Port Adelaide.

We were in Beijing on 21 July 2017 when the central government specified further limitations on investments by domestic companies in certain sectors, namely, real estate and sports. It was the headline story on the front page of *China Daily,* a government-run newspaper. Clearly, this was going to be an issue. There were further references to 'dubious overseas investment projects in some sectors, such as real estate and ... sports'.

The oft-cited example was of a Chinese businessman who made an 'ego' investment in AC Milan. In Australia, the impact on the real-estate market was discussed and understood, but the impact on sports was ignored. Port Adelaide may well have been the only Australian business impacted by the government deterrence of investment in sports clubs.

During the second half of 2017, these policies slowly strangled several conversations that had hitherto appeared positive. An existing sponsor, who had months earlier signed a significant agreement, was placed under investigation. An intermediary was jailed. We were perhaps slow to understand and respond to some challenges but did take steps to register a company in China: a joint venture between Port Adelaide and Shanghai CRED, which would allow us to be paid in China. But the process took time and was not complete until early 2019.

Meanwhile, Port Adelaide Football Club did what was required to make the 2017 season finals while failing to beat other teams in the top eight. The second Showdown was a reality check. The Crows were exceptional on a day of horrendous weather. We struggled to get the ball out of our back half, making me wonder just how good we were. In the three years I had worked at Port Adelaide, we had won just a single Showdown (the first of 2015).

The season over, the club focused on making 2018 a resounding success. We wanted to build on a successful inaugural match in China. Much to our chagrin, the AFL insisted we would once again play Gold Coast Suns. We did not realise this at the time, but the decision was near fatal in respect to the viability of playing an annual match in China. A second game between Port Adelaide and Gold Coast, at around the same time of year and at the same stadium, was never going to capture the interest of AFL followers.

Tensions were also emerging between the governments of Australia and China. Australia's approach was made more problematic by frictions within the Coalition Government. The positive energy evident during Turnbull's first trip to China in 2016, when he announced Port Adelaide's intention to play a game in China during AWIC, was evaporating. China was changing, quickly. And views in Australia with respect to the bilateral relationship were being formed in a highly political context.

When Li and Turnbull next met, at the 31st ASEAN Summit in Manila in October 2017, China's Premier warmly recalled their day at the football in Sydney and mentioned that he had a photo marking the occasion in his room, each wearing their respective scarfs. From late 2017, however, tensions between the two governments ran high. In December, 10 consecutive editions of our national daily newspaper carried a negative headline about China on the front page. Requests for visas had been refused for Cabinet ministers, as well as the head of the Department of Foreign Affairs and Trade, Frances Adamson.

The sum of policy settings in China, the state of the bilateral relationship, and the lack of excitement surrounding a second match against the Gold Coast in Shanghai presented us with a challenge. But we remained steadfast in our commitment to our objectives, and to our desire to be consistent in our approach to the Australia–China bilateral – which appeared to be in freefall.

On 19 April 2018, exactly one month prior to the game, Cheng Jingye, China's ambassador to Australia, gave an exclusive interview. In the story that appeared on the front page of the *Australian* he complained about 'systematic, irresponsible, negative remarks and comments regarding China'.

The tensions clearly impacted several conversations underway with SOEs. The breakdown of one discussion particularly stung. The prolonged conversations that had led us to Beijing in January had broken down, just when an incredible outcome had appeared to be within our grasp. The SOE was the biggest power corporation in the world; with 1.5 million employees internationally, it ranked second in the Fortune 500 pecking order. We had been introduced to them as early as May 2015, through Andrew Day. Denis Way and Peter Phillips, our friends in Hong Kong, had been instrumental in making and developing this connection. What we believed to be the largest deal in the history of the AFL, which would have delivered a modern, world-class training facility to the Alberton Oval Precinct, was an unrealised vision.

I suspect the reasons the deal failed were not due to a change of heart of the senior directors of the SOE's international business development division. Their headquarters in Beijing unequivocally reflected the power (both electrical and diplomatic) of the state and, yes, the Chinese Communist Party. Sit at a meeting at a long table inside that building, and you were sitting in a chamber where the real power in the Middle Kingdom arced and crackled.

The senior directors, the Chinese executives at the top of this monolith, were wonderful men and women to deal with. Promise and I loved talking with them, and KT developed a rapport with their most senior internationally facing executive, who regularly came to Australia for board meetings at each of their part-owned subsidiaries. This executive wanted our co-operation to culminate in the fully funded Alberton Oval Precinct redevelopment. This executive had expressed his personal agreement.

I felt as though we had gone about this the right way. Patiently. Start then pause then start again. But it wasn't enough. Political tension between Beijing and Canberra made sports diplomacy an afterthought. Such are the obstacles, traps and tests placed in the way of sports pioneers seeking new frontiers and 'clear air'. As the insurmountable barrier became increasingly apparent as the months went by, it gave further notice that this would be a year to forget.

For the past 10 years and particularly during my time at Port Adelaide, I was accompanied by the most wonderful friend. In 2008, on a visit to a pound while working in politics, I came across a mongrel Labrador and was told he would be destroyed later in the day. I asked Sally is I could Leo home, and he had been with us ever since. He was with me each morning for our morning run and slept at my feet as I finished off work in the evening. In March 2018, he was diagnosed with lymphoma.

A course of chemotherapy at The University of Adelaide's Roseworthy Campus delivered another nine beautiful months. This time was a gift. We ran more than ever, and he stayed by my side as the nights got longer and the search for solutions became urgent. In November, suddenly and over just a few days, Leo's condition worsened dramatically, and he died. He was a great mate.

The Year of the Dog really was a dog of a year.

14 Silver linings

Flashpoint … He's floating on air now, Stevie Motlop.

Commentator of Showdown 45

The first Showdown of 2018 was played the week before the game in Shanghai. It was the most memorable game I had experienced as an employee of Port Adelaide Football Club. It was also the beginning of a string of events that will shape the future of our China project.

As was the case the previous year, workload in weeks and months preceding the now annual match in China was unrelenting. A few weeks before the Showdown, I agreed to a request from Pamela Murphy, a member of our China Power Club coterie group, to meet a Chinese businessman who was visiting Adelaide. Port Adelaide is a big family, and everyone wants to help, but unless one is discerning about the introductions you accept, you will spend your life in meetings. But Pamela is a trusted friend. Zack was visiting his daughter who was about to graduate from The University of Adelaide. It seemed like the right thing to do.

So, I met 'Zack' Wang and his daughter 'June' at the Port Club. We talked about his plans in Australia, and those of his daughter. Zack was the chairman of Kailai Capital and wanted to list his company in Australia. June had spent three years studying in Adelaide. She loved it here and hoped to stay following her graduation. I talked to Zack about Port's involvement in China.

Zack was interested in our business platform. I mentioned Kogent. A small South Australian business, Kogent had spent almost eight years on R&D and had just taken the first orders for its water purification unit. Kogent had developed a product that purified water many times faster than its nearest competitor on the market and needed capital to keep up with the recent explosion in demand. Zack agreed to return to meet Andrew Townsend of Kogent, so I suggested they meet on Saturday 12 May so he could also catch a game. It was the day of the first Showdown of 2018.

Following a fruitful meeting at a hotel across the river, I took Zack and June to the game. When you have been to every PAFC home game for several years, you sometimes forget how magical the experience can be. Adelaide Oval must be the most beautiful place in the world to watch sport, and the Showdown is the most passionate of all sporting events in South Australia.

People oft refer to the magic and deeper meaning of sport, to the point of describing its spiritual dimension in religious terms. The sense of community, shared purpose and devotion are easy comparisons to make. Then the pre-game ritual gives way to the first bounce, and the experience becomes more dynamic and less predictable. A good game – a game well played or nail-bitingly close – is a captivating mixture of competition, drama, and art. The first Showdown of 2018 had all these elements.

Port Adelaide won the match by five points. Behind four

goals to one at quarter-time and eight goals to four at half-time, Port Adelaide powered back into the game in the third term, helped by the sublime Robbie Gray who kicked five goals. The stadium was buzzing. But the best was yet to come. With Port Adelaide heading towards victory, Adelaide surged back in time-on, kicking three consecutive goals and taking the lead with less than a minute to go. My new friends could feel how important the outcome was by the tension on my face! Somehow, after the centre bounce, the ball came to Motlop in a goal-scoring position and he kicked truly. Euphoria. Port Adelaide had won its first Showdown since 2015.

Our house is in Rosewater. Any train travelling on the Outer Harbor line after a Port Adelaide victory is a happy place to be. As this was a home Showdown, the walk from the Oval to the train station was particularly enjoyable. I once heard footballer Greg Anderson talk about the atmosphere in the heartland on the night of a SANFL Port Adelaide win against Norwood, in the 1980s. He would leave Alberton Oval and on the way home, see lights still shining on verandas of local homes illuminating Port Adelaide paraphernalia left out to show pride in the team representing their community. 'We didn't feel better than the folk in Burnside too often – but we did every time we won against Norwood.' Winning a Showdown, I reflected on the train home, had much the same effect.

When I arrived home, I completed preparations for my flight the next morning. I received an email from Zack. He signed off: 'We Are Port Adelaide.' It took two years to complete the deal between Kailai and Kogent (and even now I understand there are challenges transferring funds due to a tightening of regulations), during which there were ample opportunities and reasons to abort, but the relationship formed around sport remained strong and the two companies stayed the course.

At around 5 am the next morning, I was at the airport with others who had worked over many months preparing for the second-ever Australian Rules football match in China. We were on our way. As we were playing against the same team, in the same venue, at around the same time of year as the inaugural event, the game didn't attract as much attention from the football media. But in many ways, the week demonstrated the progress that had been made, painstakingly, over the intervening 12 months.

Port Adelaide had from the beginning wanted its engagement in China to provide a platform that would help bring the people, businesses and governments of Australia and China closer together. Even though the game in Shanghai failed to recapture the excitement of the inaugural game, it was able to bring together people, businesses, and governments to shared experiences, knowledge and wealth. Everyone was better for the experience, and no amount of superficial commentary about a few empty seats in the stands will diminish the value of what is being developed.

We remained firm in the belief that there is merit in using sport for a higher purpose. But it is important for our business to develop new connections and to present ourselves strongly in markets that had not traditionally been exposed to the Port Adelaide Football Club. It takes time to fully realise the potential of new frontiers. As Gui once said, it is normal for pioneers to feel alone. They are the ones with the courage to go where others dare not. And in the days leading into the Shanghai 2018 match, it felt as though we were a lot closer than we had been 12 months earlier.

We visited two schools during the week. On Thursday, we visited Red Balloon Kindergarten where the children were introduced to Australia through our most popular sport. The school did an exercise routine to the tune of 'The Power to Win', a basic football clinic followed. As the club's CFO Shane Smith said, the smiles are just as big on Chinese kids as they are on Australian kids when they have a football in their hands. The following day, the recently elected premier of South Australia, Steven Marshall, attended the Bile Middle School to announce the first 'Power Footy Study' tour, which was to take place in July 2018. The idea of encouraging Power Footy participants to travel to Adelaide for a study tour had long been attractive. This opportunity to interact and the understanding that will grow are fundamental to the health of the bilateral relationship, which will inevitably be influenced by domestic audiences.

Port Adelaide's efforts to strengthen ties between Australian and Chinese businesses had evolved. The day before the game, Port Adelaide co-hosted a business-to-business event with the Chinese Chamber of International Commerce (CCOIC). Australia's Minister for Trade, Tourism and Investment, Steven Ciobo MP, attended the event and witnessed the signing of an agreement between Kailai Capital and Kogent. Referring to the 'unlikely combination of sport and business', Mike Smith reported in the *Australian Financial Review* that 'Port Adelaide Football Club, which played an annual AFL match in Shanghai last month, said it connected the two companies as part of its new business program designed to help Australian companies do business in China'.

So, less than one week after their introduction (on the day of Zack's Showdown experience) he signed an agreement on behalf of Kailai Capital to invest an eight-figure sum in a small Australian business producing water purification units that will seriously improve the standard of water for millions of people. Letters of Intent were also signed between importers and exporters. These outcomes deepened our belief that sport can be a platform through which businesses can meet and explore opportunities in a friendly and credible context.

Does Port Adelaide have a direct role to play in facilitating trade and investment opportunities? Probably not. It is too far removed from our core business and core expertise. Within twelve months, we moved away from the Business Platform program, finding it a diversion from the main game. In the course of creating something out of nothing, however, you're going to make mistakes. We were having a crack.

Importantly, we were developing an important platform that could be used for business and diplomacy. Sports diplomacy – the idea that sport can be used as a diplomatic instrument to improve relations between two governments – is a hard thesis to test. Circumstance plays a role in deciding whether a sporting event becomes sports diplomacy. In May 2018, few were writing positive stories about the Australia–China relationship.

On 18 April, Chinese Ambassador Cheng had raised his concerns about the bilateral but said there was 'huge potential' for expanded cooperation and said that no visas of high-ranking Australian officials had been rejected. We received a phone call from the AFL. Minister Ciobo had been refused a visa on multiple occasions, and there were questions as to whether he would be successful if he applied for a visa to attend the game. We communicated these concerns to the Chinese Embassy and were informed this matter could be settled by an informal request. If the response to the informal request was positive, the outcome of any formal visa request would be a foregone conclusion. And it was. An opinion piece I penned was published in the business section of the *Australian* on Thursday 3 May. It argued the match in Shanghai would be an appropriate forum for the commencement of the thawing of relations. It also suggested that we will only realise the potential of the bilateral relationship if it is founded on 'friendship, understanding and trust' – the three words that appeared on the banner players ran through prior to the game.

Rowan Callick, once again in the *Australian,* asked: 'Would Trade Minister Ciobo be welcome again? The extensive contacts between Port Adelaide and Chinese officialdom that are necessary to organise such an event provided an excellent opportunity to test the acceptability of Ciobo's participation ... The green light ensured no loss of face on either side ... and ... marked something of a re-stabilisation of relations at the official level.'

At the same time the players ran onto the ground and through the banner, representatives from the governments of Australia and China met in the bosom of the renamed 'Adelaide Arena at Jiangwan Stadium' for an official government-to-government meeting – the first to be held for over eight months. In an old stadium and at a game some had dismissed as insignificant or a sideshow, two governments met and discussed their differences. On the front of the banner the players breached on their way onto the field were the words: Proud of the Past. Confident in the Future. A version of these words would become our motto in 2020, the year of our 150th anniversary.

For those involved, the experience of Shanghai 2018 did not feel the same as that exciting first journey. Yet, in some ways it was more meaningful. The execution of the game was seamless. The brilliant work of Shane Smith and Jacinta Alexander made sure of that. There was a level of trust and understanding between the local authorities and the AFL that had been absent a year earlier. More local people attended the game, either business leaders networking in corporate hospitality or *Power Footy* participants watching the game with their parents and classmates. Businesses had come together for mutual benefit, and governments had started talking again. And Port Adelaide remained undefeated on Chinese soil.

15 An international education

Ideas are art.

Marcel Duchamp

After having worked into a strong position, sitting fourth on the ladder with 11 wins and four losses, our 2018 season started to fall away following a nine-point loss to Fremantle in Perth. A further loss to GWS was followed by a convincing victory against Western Bulldogs, leaving the season in a delicate position leading into Showdown 46. The Crows had experienced a disastrous season but could salvage some pride by pushing Port Adelaide into a precarious position. Which they ultimately did in another pulsating match defined by the Jenkins' honest post-match analysis of a point that was awarded a goal: 'My grandma raised me not to tell fibs ...'

Port Adelaide was hosting Jincheng Group at the Showdown. This strong privately owned company turned over billions of dollars each year, with strong interests in real estate, aged care, and education. The group indirectly came into our orbit through introductions made by Graeme Willis, a Port Adelaide fan based in Zhejiang Province. We had travelled to Zhejiang a couple of times to speak with prospects, including Alibaba and Holley Group. On the eve of the match in Shanghai, we had signed an agreement to execute *Power Footy* into Entel Education Group's schools.

We had launched the *Power Footy* program in China in late 2016. Like many things, the program was beautiful in its vision, and difficult in its execution! To promote the first AFL match due to be played in Shanghai in 2017, KT wanted to take our leadership group to Shanghai and interact with local schoolchildren. He held the vision of busloads of schoolkids descending on a central location where our guys would be training. At that time, we hadn't even considered school programs in China. But that changed.

By 2018, there were about 4000 participants of the program we branded *Power Footy*. As we were not in the business of game development – which is the AFL's responsibility – we believed we could potentially sell the branded program. It was also an important way of building an audience for games we hoped would become an annual event in China. In time, we narrowed the design of the program's expansion to focus on schools with an international orientation. If students were contemplating higher education in Australia, an understanding of our sport would be a great way of learning about our culture, society, and history.

In July 2018, we also signed a three-year agreement with The University of Adelaide. A member of the Group of Eight, the Dean of the Faculty of Professions, Christopher Findlay, believed in our vision of building a community between Australia and China through our indigenous game. The agreement signed between the two parties reflected the university's desire to increase student enrolments from China, and to leverage our network to bring greater opportunities for its students to undertake meaningful internships. But there was also a strong philosophical commitment to the idea of enriching the student experience and developing a strong connection with the local community.

There is an interesting history to Chinese students in Australia. Between 1920 and 1925 the Chinese Consul organised passports for around 400 Chinese students to study in Australia, successfully petitioning the Australian Government to issue visas. An invitation was made to the Australian Government to reciprocate; however, it was declined, and the program only lasted five years. Attracting Chinese students to Australia become a priority in the 21st century when the economic benefit of international education had become apparent.

There is some experience in Australia of programs designed to achieve human as well as economic benefit through international education. Australia was a willing and active participant in the Colombo Plan, which started in 1951. It was the first meaningful attempt by the Australian Government to participate in a region-wide program designed to use education as a tool for engagement with Asia.

Several aspects of the program enhanced the quality and volume of interactions between international students and the local community: for example, visiting students were placed in Australian communities and homes for the duration of their stay, which was illuminating and meaningful for both students and hosts. It was a beautiful vision lost in the cynical, economistic modern times.

But interacting with international students was one of the first initiatives of our engagement strategy. Since 2014,

Port Adelaide has regularly invited Chinese students living in Adelaide to its home games. In 2016, we partnered with a member of the China Power Club, AIES, which was owned and managed by avid Port Adelaide supporters Roland and Jessi Tan. We wanted to enhance the experience of students attending our games. To do so, we arranged a presentation about footy in their city office before each game. Following the presentation, the students joined other supporters in the 'March from the Mall' – a pre-match ritual in which Port Adelaide's supporters congregate at Rundle Mall before walking to Adelaide Oval together.

Although Port Adelaide had been actively involved in education in both Australia and China, we needed to bring together our institutional partners on both sides to develop a meaningful and commercially viable program. The inbound delegation from Jincheng Group, which included its Chairman Wu Wanglou and several general managers, was an opportunity to establish something of lasting significance. And from 2 to 4 August, their program included meetings with Chancellor of Adelaide University Kevin Scarce, Premier Stephen Marshall, and the Federal Minister for Education, Senator Birmingham. It was an impressive program, demonstrating the central role of sport to Australian – particularly South Australian – society.

Yet despite this program of activity, and the number of meetings that took place over several days, it was not until we watched the Showdown together that a lasting connection was made between Port Adelaide Football Club and Jincheng Group. As professional, measured and calm as you wish to remain, in what is essentially a commercial program designed for mutual commercial benefit, it is impossible, I think, to experience a game between Port Adelaide and Adelaide and deny the raw emotion the game elicits.

The second Showdown of 2018, like the first, was one for the ages. But this time, the result didn't fall our way. And, in the context of the season, it was a significant result. It was clear, as we shared a meal with the Jincheng team after the game, that a connection based on something more than the potential for mutual benefit had been established. The disappointment and hurt at losing a Showdown was difficult to hide, and there was empathy in the interaction over dinner. We sensed we were in trouble, and subsequent results in the 2018 season confirmed this.

This deeper connection was important in the year that was to follow. Jincheng Group's desire to partner with Port Adelaide was predicated on the successful connection between itself and the University of Adelaide to deliver a foundation course in its high schools. This was a complicated, prolonged, at times difficult negotiation. Without a strong commitment from all parties, an agreement would not be reached. Promise Xu was a star, holding these conversations together.

In 2020, when the impact of COVID-19 on Australia became clear, the chairman of Jincheng wrote to KT. The letter made apparent the depth of a relationship that had been assiduously built. He noted that '... this is no longer a challenge that any country can solve on its own, but a challenge that needs all of us to work together ...', before employing a quote that has been attributed to Seneca: 'We are waves of the same sea, leaves of the same tree, flowers of the same garden.' Then, he affirmed 'We will stand with Port Adelaide Football Club, to support each other through the hard time.' Which company doesn't dream of seeing such sentiments, in a moment of real need?

Back to the days leading into Shanghai 2019 when the final steps towards an agreement were confirmed, triggering a commercial partnership between Port Adelaide and Jincheng Group. This partnership will be a lucrative, long-term relationship, based on shared intentions, mutual benefit, and friendship. The delegation from the Jincheng Group demonstrates how sport in Australia can be an effective and important ancillary to formal business meetings. Instead of sitting opposite, you sit alongside your potential business partner. You wear the same scarf. You connect.

Port Adelaide would like to replicate the likes of this program. We believe in the human, as well as the economic, potential of these relationships. As I wrote in an opinion piece in *InDaily* in December 2018, 'too many international students have a narrow experience of Australia, with their network confined to their respective linguistic, national or ethnic groups. They are not embraced by the broader community, but instead remain isolated'. What better platform than sport to welcome international students into the Australian community?

Our indigenous sport is a carrier of Australian cultural values. To experience it is to better understand Australia, both good and bad. On a more common level, being able to talk about football also provides an 'ice-breaker' in Australian workplaces or bars. It encourages more meaningful interactions with the local community, which can have a transformative effect. Sport puts all members of the community on the same playing field, as equal participants.

In Australia, there is a distance between our appetite

to receive more students from overseas and our sense of responsibility to the growing number of students who arrive on our shores. The confluence of pressure, isolation and loneliness can have tragic consequences. Less tragic consequences include graduating a group of socially marginalised people who leave Australia having completed their degrees with only superficial experience of our country. The learning experience is also made difficult by moderate English-language proficiency.

We continued to invite Chinese students to our remaining games in 2018, as our season was expunged before the disbelieving eyes of the Port Adelaide faithful. The week following the Showdown we lost to West Coast by four points, thanks to a goal kicked after the siren. Eerily similar to the last act of the 2017 Elimination Final, I looked across to Kochie, KT and other board members and knew our season was over. The last thing that was needed, at that critical point, was a reminder of the pain of bygone seasons. The manner of the losses to Collingwood and Essendon were depressing and predicable. It made clear the need for dramatic change, which soon arrived.

In early 2019, Port Adelaide launched its International Students Program on the roof of Urbanest on North Terrace. A few months earlier, a Chinese student had jumped from the same spot, taking his life. We are serious about our commitment to sport as a platform to achieve transformative change in people's lives. We want to use its magic to overcome the disconnection between Australia and China. And we hope others continue to support this vision.

16 A new Day

'Get me that moon!'
says the child,
in tears.
Issa

The summer that separated the unfulfilled promise of 2018 with the winter of 2019 was tense. The football department understood that changes were essential and made hard decisions. These changes were broadly unpopular. Talented players were discarded, and faith was placed in the next generation. Traditions were broken when Tom Jonas and Oli Wines were announced co-captains. This was divisive within the club's administration and was unpopular with members and supporters.

As a former professional athlete, I believed the administration of a club cannot, under any circumstances, impose its will on those responsible for on-ground success. Such a measure would produce an irreparable fissure of trust between the sporting and administrative arms. Confidence must be placed in those responsible for on-field success for a professional sporting club to succeed. This issue was hugely divisive, particularly after the mediocre results of previous seasons.

There were also changes made at an administrative level. Darren Cahill and Gavin Wanganeen were added to the board. Darren understands international sport and was supportive of what we were doing in China. I knew Gavin from his involvement in Power Community Limited. With his accession to the board, this Port Adelaide champion had gone full circle. I remember watching him during his breakout season in the SANFL in 1990.

A board committee had been created to focus on the club's engagement in China. Two outsider experts had been invited to join. Danny Armstrong, who had set up the Commonwealth Bank in Vietnam then National Australia Bank (NAB) in China, and Andrew Day, a Port Adelaide supporter who had been CEO of Hastings and came with a rich experience of attracting investment from China. These were significant decisions for Port Adelaide. And the promise of ongoing progress and personal development was reassuring.

So, as the football department prepared for a season of intense scrutiny, having taken bold but unpopular decisions, it was also important for Port Adelaide's members and fans to see the direct commercial benefit of our engagement in China. Following two years of unanticipated achievement, from the initial commercial and broadcasting agreements with CRED and CCTV to the announcement then execution of the first game in China, great progress had been made. But it was time to consolidate, and to rebound quickly from a challenging year in 2018.

The foundations of our annual AFL match in Shanghai were strengthening. Port Adelaide had signed a three-year agreement for St Kilda to play the game in China. This was significant because another match against Gold Coast in Shanghai might well have killed the concept. With St Kilda, the Victorian Government became strongly implicated in the project – even if they only modestly contributed to the funding of the game itself. By now the AFL had also developed a stronger interest in China.

These were welcome changes, but they also constituted a challenge to Port Adelaide's close identification with China. The Victorian Government invested significant resources into its global engagement. It has a representative office in Shanghai that accommodates over a dozen staff and would naturally want the Victorian club to be successful. Victoria is also the home of the Australia China Business Council (ACBC). At the time, its president, John Brumby, and CEO, Helen Sawczak, were Victorian. ACBC strongly supported the vision of taking our sport to China.

And, of course, the AFL is a Victorian organisation. Having committed negligible resources to the first two games in China, apart from Dave Stevenson who worked for them as a consultant in 2018, it had now made a strategic decision to invest in business development in China. It recruited fluent Mandarin speaker Tom Parker from Bastion and decided to put people on the ground in China. There was a risk that Port Adelaide would be overwhelmed by these well-resourced organisations.

South Australia, by contrast, had opened a representative office in Shanghai in November 2018 – but as of early 2019, the office was staffed by just one person. The network of South Australians in China was relatively small. Larger brands entering the Australian market would want to maximise its exposure in the larger markets of Melbourne and Sydney. There were no natural advantages on which to call. We had to be, as Paul Keating would say, a little bit clever.

The day before the first game of the season, the board's China committee met for the first time. After four years, a more refined strategy was being consolidated. The 2019 season started in style, with a convincing victory against Melbourne at the MCG. I went to Melbourne to watch the game with my 16-month-old son Theodore, as well as my father and sister. Three generations watching a game together; how wonderfully Australian.

Theodore barely made it to half-time but the look of wonderment in his eyes as the players entered the field was like sunshine on a rainy day. From Port Adelaide's perspective, what a game! Melbourne kicked the first three goals, but we steadied, then excelled. The style the team had developed during the off-season was markedly different: fluent, daring, exciting. The new generation had talent and played with confidence and personality.

Slowly, the foundation stones of an enduring successful strategy were being put in place. CRED had extended its agreement with Port Adelaide for a further five years. Our agreement with The University of Adelaide was less than one year into a three-year agreement, and the deliverance of a foundation course for Jincheng Group would trigger a five-year agreement with the latter. We were negotiating an agreement with PWC, which was ultimately signed shortly after returning from China. These deals represented new revenue streams without attrition of traditional assets like signage at the ground, or a logo on the team jumper.

This was not always well understood to our members and supporter base. By design, these sponsorships were not intended to take traditional assets, leaving them to be sold from within our traditional market. It was, in fact, the principal reason why we were in China: to rise above the congested landscape of Australian sporting clubs and find new revenue streams. We had developed a platform that was of value to significant companies willing to sign long-term agreements.

Andrew Day and I travelled to China together in February 2019, to start discussions with a new suite of large companies with existing interests in Australia. For the most part, the people we spoke to were cautious. Some were aware of the limits placed on companies investing in foreign sporting clubs – particularly 'football' clubs. Our sport continued to be confused with soccer.

Others were cautious about investing in Australia at all. They believed the Australian Government had an inconsistent, and overly political regulatory environment. Why would you invest in renewables in Australia as opposed to Europe, where governments predictably and consistently followed the Paris Accord? This observation was made by a senior executive from CNIC Corporation while we enjoyed a working dinner in Hong Kong. Looking across the harbour, it was obvious that China could invest anywhere – and like any smart investment, there is risk associated with an unpredictable regulatory framework.

This trip did open some opportunities. As the year progressed, our confidence swelled as we developed a pipeline of conversations with large, significant Chinese companies such as SAIC Motor, formerly Shanghai Automotive Industry Corporation. Some of the relationships developed on this trip helped us navigate these significant organisations. On field and off field, we felt we were making progress towards our ultimate goals, but the patience of our supporters, and perhaps some board members, was running out. It was also critical we found a deeper purpose to the game in China for it to remain relevant.

17 Festival of Australia

I assume you're acquainted with Sisyphus and his rock collection?
Extract of email from Michael Clifton to author

I always thought that maybe Sisyphus just didn't believe hard enough. Anyway, having pushed an (admittedly lighter) rock up a hill in 2016, I'm inspired to keep pushing for the moment.
Extract of email from author to Michael Clifton

If the game in Shanghai in 2019 was not considered a success, it would likely mark the end of the experiment of playing AFL matches in China.

Following the second game against Gold Coast in 2018, two things were clear. The first was that if the AFL obliged us to play the same team again, the concept would be killed. The second was that the game needed to serve a broader purpose, to promote Australia in China. This had always been Kochie's vision. He understood that Australian football did not have a resonance in China, but Australian lifestyle, education, food, and wine were attractive to a local audience.

We tried a form of this in 2017, but on a small scale and on the day of the game. It was difficult for us to organise this sort of activation without help. It was not our area of expertise and the exigencies of government approvals were great. In the second year, we tried business-matching events. Again, our attempt to merge business and sporting interests required expertise well outside the core business of football clubs, thus produced modest outcomes.

Throughout the period, we had also promoted the game as a means of serving diplomatic interests; a moment in which representatives of our two governments could come together in a friendly context. It was here that we had some success, even if success was largely dependent on circumstance. We had not landed on an effective formula, but we knew the annual match in China could serve a broader set of interests.

The reality was that government and business was better placed to do all of these things. It was better placed to promote Australian food and wine. It was better placed to develop business-matching programs. And it was certainly better placed to decide whether the game was an appropriate backdrop for diplomatic exchange. We needed to encourage the Federal Government to consider the AFL as an anchor to a broader program. Luckily, within government, there were people thinking along similar lines. Such a program made sense and was critical to the long-term viability of the AFL match in China.

Australia Week In China, a biennial event, was considered a success in 2014 and 2016. Existing tensions between the two governments meant it did not happen in 2018 – and there was no talk of a fresh concept to replace it. Programs which encouraged trade, investment, tourism, cultural and sporting exchange did not need to exist in isolation. An holistic approach that intermingled cultural and commercial exchange was worth pursuing, particularly in a country Australia considered a 'customer', rather than a friend.

In retrospect, it was fanciful to think that Port Adelaide Football Club could contribute ideas and inspiration to a new concept of promoting Australia in China. Tensions between

Australia and China, a looming Federal election, rejection of AWIC – all contributed to a cautious response to advocacy for a new festival anchored by an AFL match.

A sense of futile toil was not helped by two trips to Canberra for meetings on this subject. Meetings had been arranged at the last minute with advisers from the offices of the Minister for Foreign Affairs, and Minister for Trade. As the meetings were arranged on the first morning of a sitting week, there were no direct flights to Canberra and alternate routes were exorbitantly expensive (these were austere times at Port Adelaide!). Without thinking, I jumped in a car and drove to Canberra. Which I didn't mind, until I hit a 'roo as I approached Canberra at dusk, and went flying off the road, lucky to miss a couple of trees at speed.

Another senior bureaucrat compared our advocacy for the idea with Sisyphus, the Greek king punished by pushing a large rock up a hill for eternity, the rock rolling back each time it neared the top. There was some encouragement from Michael Clifton, who analysed the timing of the game and noted it would not clash with the international program of summits, and in late May was sufficiently distant from the handing down of the Federal Budget for Australian ministers – even prime ministers – to travel.

In parallel, a small, dedicated team within Austrade were considering a modest program of activity in various Chinese cities as part of their annual food and beverage business plan. By coincidence, Wine Australia had scheduled their annual China Roadshow to finish in Shenzhen only a few days before the AFL game. The idea of developing a broader program of partner-led activities promoted under a single umbrella gathered momentum inside Austrade. Soon, the planets would align.

These meetings, and numerous others, indicated support for a new concept was increasing. The growing consensus was inspired by a couple of champions who believed strongly in the vision. Trade Commissioner Karen Surmon, a South Australian working in Austrade's Shanghai office, was incredibly supportive and mentioned the planned 'Australia Festival Regional Roadshow'. We discussed linking this initiative with other events hosted by AustCham (an organisation supporting Australian business in China), and the states of Victoria and South Australia. Karen is an inspiring person, taking on thankless workloads and getting things done. Without champions like her, and the small group of colleagues working tirelessly, the effort from Port Adelaide would have been futile.

KT, Dave Stevenson from the AFL and I met with Senator Birmingham, Minister for Trade, Tourism and Investment. Kochie and I met with Austrade's CEO, Dr Stephanie Fahey, in Sydney. Andrew Day and I met with Ambassador Adams in Beijing to discuss the idea, a meeting attended by Daniel Boyer, Austrade's General Manager for Greater China. Liu Bing, Austrade's Senior Trade Commissioner in Shanghai, was another champion of the concept.

I met with Austrade staff in Shanghai, Adelaide, Canberra, Sydney and Beijing. There were positive signs. In November, speaking from the China International Import Expo (CIIE) in Shanghai, Minister Birmingham stated on Sky News: 'Now we will have a look at what our opportunities are for the future in terms of whether it's Australia Week in China, whether it's a different type of format that piggybacks off this event, off the annual AFL match that's now going to be committed over the next few years ...'

Rowan Callick wrote a very helpful piece in the *Australian* in January, in which he quoted Simon Birmingham. Callick further noted 'even a modest success for such an audacious project would place us potentially ahead of our competitors, and would potentially do much to deepen demand for our goods and services'.

Support was growing. There were champions in government, in government agencies, in the media, and in industry. Austrade pressed on, uniting a growing list of government and industry partners to support a two-week program of activities across China, culminating in game day. AustCham wrote in support of the broader concept, as did the Winemakers Federation of Australia, the Australia China Business Council, the Australia China Council, AustCham Shanghai and ShineWing. Heavyweights such as businessman and former minister Warwick Smith wrote in support. We heard that a decision had been made in favour of this concept, with commitment to financially support the game. A pre-budget announcement was suggested. There was some last-minute wrangling between government agencies as to which one would foot the bill, but the rock had nearly reached the top of the hill.

Which, according to legend, is when it starts rolling back down! I made a second trip to Canberra in early March. I was sure to arrange the meetings and book the flights well in advance. About an hour into the flight, there was a loud crack and oxygen masks fell from the ceiling. The plane was in rapid descent. I am scared of flying, but for a few moments was in denial. The scene was too familiar, this had been a recurring nightmare since I was a child. The passenger next to me screamed hysterically as the plane descended 15,000 feet in a minute or so, but then it steadied and diverted to Melbourne. Would we ever make it to the top of the mountain?

On 30 March 2019, outside the Southern Plaza at Adelaide Oval, Simon Birmingham and Kochie stood together and announced the Festival of Australia, to be held in May 2019 culminating in the match on June 2, as well as the Federal Government's support for the AFL match in China over the next three years. The planets had aligned. The press conference was held hours before our first home match of the season, against Carlton, which we won after a dour struggle. We had managed to push the rock to the top of the hill and had secured critical support from the Federal Government for the next three years for the AFL match in Shanghai.

A seven-point loss to an injury-depleted Richmond at Adelaide Oval frustrated. The next week, I was in Perth when we dismantled premier West Coast at Optus Arena. Leading 9.9 to 2.2 at half-time, playing with incredible intensity, there were signs that a team and culture was being constructed that could compete for premierships, which is, after all, the club's raison d'être.

I took Theodore to the game in Perth. I was also at Adelaide Oval (without Theodore) when our injury-depleted team lost the first Showdown of the year despite getting back in the game with five straight goals in the last quarter. Port Adelaide arrived in Shanghai with five wins and five losses, and plenty of rocks to push up hills.

18 Building

I cannot fiddle, but I can make a great state of a small city.

Themistocles

On a beautiful warm day, Port Adelaide once again did the business in Shanghai. And, once again, we lost the next game, this time to Fremantle in Perth. This confirmed a pattern of dominance in China, followed by a loss the following round. Once again, some chose to ridicule the project on account of sparsely populated pockets of 'Adelaide Arena at Jiangwan Stadium'.

In 2019, the event was superbly executed. PAFC's project lead, CFO Shane Smith, and Jacinta Alexander delivered an international sporting event that was worthy of its positioning as a flagship event in the new Festival of Australia program. The Gala Dinner attracted an audience of around 600 guests, each paying around $600. It was said that Gillon described the room as the most high-powered in Australian sport, following the prestigious pre-game function in the Olympic Room on AFL grand final day.

Less than 48 hours after being sworn in as Minister for Youth and Sport, Senator Richard Colbeck arrived in time to make a speech at the Gala Dinner and attend the match the following day. The inaugural Festival of Australia – a program of 43 events in 10 Chinese cities across two weeks – attracted a digital reach of over 90 million, and was considered an outstanding success.

Port Adelaide's engagement in China is a commercially motivated strategy. We sought to attract new partners and develop new revenue streams. In 2019, the game, now part of the Festival of Australia, was part of a formal government-endorsed platform and was fulfilling the original vision we had for it: to assist Port Adelaide to capture the attention of a new audience of influential people.

For a season that was ultimately disappointing, 2019 produced some special personal moments. In round one, I watched Port Adelaide triumph against Melbourne at the MCG with my dad by my side and Theodore in my arms. Even sweeter, I saw our boys decimate West Coast in Perth, sitting alongside my Western Australian, Eagles-supporting father-in-law. The night match we played against Geelong, in Round 14, was the best memory of all.

Following a letdown in Perth against Fremantle, Port Adelaide returned to Adelaide Oval and produced another electric display, defeating Geelong by 11 points in front of 37,726 fans – one of whom was my nan. Nan was born in a house on Judith Street in Pennington. Her mother was born in a house on Charles Street in Pennington. Nan was married in Alberton Methodist Church and her husband, a jockey, trained at the Cheltenham racecourse.

An avid football lover just turned 93 years old she had never seen Port Adelaide play at Adelaide Oval in the AFL – until that night. Family from Red Hill, as well as Mum, my sister Loire, Sally and Theodore, and Robert Blackborough were all there.

It was an incredible night to be part of the football family.

The atmosphere at the ground in the final two minutes, as Port Adelaide inched towards victory, was electric. It felt like we were heading in the right direction, united. Throughout the season, an exhilarating performance one week was often followed by a loss that once again tempered expectations. It was sometimes hard to see, and harder to trust, but something was building.

The quest to develop sustainable, alternative revenue streams from our engagement with China continued to both promise and frustrate. Pioneers never know what sits over the horizon. Soon after the game, the movement in Hong Kong posed further questions. Since our partnership with Cathay Pacific, we had a habit of travelling through Hong Kong, where we saw commercial potential and a strong network of friends.

It wasn't possible for Promise to visit Hong Kong in the second half of 2019, although I continued to do so, avoiding weekends when the troubles really started. The level of violence, on both sides, was disturbing and often vicious. The way in which these events were interpreted in the Western media focused on political freedom, but others had essentially economic interpretations for local frustration at Mainland China. With a third of marriages between locals and mainlanders, it was a complex issue with no solution in sight.

Neither Port Adelaide, nor the AFL, spoke publicly on the situation in Hong Kong – unlike the NBA. In Suzuka, where I participated on a panel about sports diplomacy at the Japanese Grand Prix, I raised this issue with Chase Carey, chief executive officer and executive chairman of the Formula One Group. He suggested it was best not to proactively engage on the issue, but it is difficult to limit the speech of athletes and administrators. I tend to agree – particularly when those athletes are taking a principled position. I couldn't help but wonder how much context or understanding sat behind the public comments that led to embarrassing retractions from the NBA.

As an important page was written in the history of modern Asia, Port Adelaide focused on consolidating the foundation that had been assiduously developed.

An important part of our value proposition was our relationship with The University of Adelaide, and we strongly believed in what this institution could deliver to education groups looking to internationalise their offering through partnerships with elite universities. The University of Adelaide is not currently ranked as high as Melbourne University, for example, or UNSW. Students and parents are also more familiar with Sydney and Melbourne, which further impacts on the relative attractiveness of Adelaide.

With the prolonged experience of negotiating an outcome with Jincheng Group, we better understood how to talk about the outstanding features of this Group of Eight universities, which has produced six of Australia's 15 Nobel Laureates. We came to understand our value, and the role of an intermediary driving benefit for partners on each side of a two-sided market.

Power Footy had become a trojan horse for our education sector business development. We had developed a foothold for *Power Footy* in Chengdu, thanks to a grant from the DFAT's Australia–China Council, and used it to develop a pipeline of local companies that might benefit from an association with Port Adelaide. If events had made the exploration of opportunities in Hong Kong more difficult, it allowed us to focus on another city with which Australia shares a certain cultural propinquity.

Australia's Consul-General to Chengdu, Christopher Lim, was incredibly supportive. On several occasions he hosted dinners in his residence for partners and prospective partners, demonstrating his commitment to deepening the cultural and commercial links between Australia and China. His knowledge of history always impressed his guests, both local and Australian.

One evening, he explained how Chengdu and Australia shared a similar tradition of migration. Migration to Sichuan in the 17th and 18th centuries was a significant population movement in Chinese history. Famines, epidemics, revolts, and massacres had reduced the population to almost nothing. Earth burnings had reduced the previously fertile soil to wasteland. Incentives were granted to farmers willing to come to Sichuan to reinstate its historic role as China's food bowl. Many others were forced to migrate, to repopulate its towns and villages. As in Australia, most people residing in Sichuan had relatively short local histories.

One of the companies that had deep commercial roots in Australia was Hope Group. We had been seeking the opportunity to connect with this group for some time, but eventually an introduction was brokered by Tim White, the impressive head of Austrade in Chengdu. Hope Group was formed in 1982 by four siblings, who then preceded to split the parent group into four groups with different sectoral and regional focuses, to be managed by each of the siblings: East Hope, West Hope, Continental Hope and New Hope. It is a behemoth.

West Hope Group had strong interests in education. It had formed Hope Education, which is on track to soon become the largest education group, in terms of both the number of students educated and number of universities owned. Following a tour of one of its university campuses, I met with Hope Education Chairman Li Tao to discuss a potential partnership.

If sometimes it feels hard to explain our value proposition as a football club operating in a sector removed from our core business, occasionally a meeting is held in which you immediately understand that your interlocking grasps the value of what you are proposing. This was such a meeting.

We had prepared well and, at the end, drew further attention to The University of Adelaide's credentials as Australia's Nobel Prize-winning institution by gifting Li Tao a personally signed copy of J.M. Coetzee's latest novel. To be successful when trying to achieve an outcome so unlikely, it pays to grasp every opportunity. At the time of writing, I wonder how many of the doors painstakingly prised open will be kept shut following the COVID crisis.

This was also the first serious meeting that featured Tony Zhang, Port Adelaide's first executive to be based in China. Former trade commissioner for the New South Wales Government, Tony became our Chief Representative for China in November 2019. With an old China hand now on the board, which was supported by a China Engagement committee and a chief representative on the ground in Shanghai, there is an organisational structure in place that will help us succeed.

19 The ticking bomb that exploded at Marvel Stadium

> *Instead of paying attention to the faces of the people passing by, I watched their feet, and all these busy types were reduced to hurrying steps – towards what? And it was clear to me that our mission was to graze the dust in search of a mystery stripped of anything serious.*
>
> Emil Goram, in *Anathemas and Admirations*

In the second half of the 2019 season, Port Adelaide oscillated between hope and despair, before it finally receded into the dominant question of the previous five years: where was it all heading? Port Adelaide fans lacked confidence that the club was heading in the right direction, on and off the field. Fans of AFL clubs equally generally lacked confidence in the guardians of the sport they hold dear.

Port Adelaide has many informal and formal supporter groups; each develop their own habits and traditions. One such group is the Alberton Crowd, which has taken to meeting at the London Tavern before home games. I was at 'the London' before the Geelong game. The place was pumping. Caitlin, Cathryn, and Phil introduced themselves and the Alberton Crowd.

One of the traditions of the Alberton Crowd is to go on an annual 'tour of duty'. Before the season, they select a game in Melbourne, and travel *en masse* to support the team. The game they selected in 2019 was our round 22 match against North Melbourne at Marvel Stadium. It isn't cheap to get to Melbourne for a game, particularly when you're a student. It is also a bloody long drive back when your team doesn't perform as you'd hoped.

It is fair to say that Port Adelaide did not perform as well as it might have on that evening. Since 2017, the number of members had decreased. Member sentiment was in freefall. We were last in the AFL for new member acquisition. We had to do better.

Confidence in our leaders was diminishing. The club was perceived to be equivocating. Winning premierships was part of our mission statement, yet between November 2018 and the end of our season in August 2019, the word 'premiership' was not used in any public statement by our Chairman, our CEO, or our coach. Words are important. They are related to intent. Did we really exist to win premierships?

Ironically, decisions made during this period show how serious we were about achieving our mission. Experienced players were traded, and talented young players like Rozee, Duursma and Butters were drafted. These decisions were made with a view of putting together a list capable of winning a premiership. It is a shame we didn't communicate this clearly.

Confidence in Port Adelaide's China engagement had also softened. We were not only getting challenged on the commercial viability of the strategy, but on its morality. In September 2019, a member emailed to say that he wouldn't renew his membership 'while the club pursues this support of China', citing concerns for its treatment of Uighurs. I met him for coffee. He had taken a principled stance, was well informed, and his concerns were justified.

I expressed my belief that engagement is the surest path to progress; isolation achieves little. And China is not the only country that infringes on human rights. It is a privilege to be involved in a club where each keeps the other honest. These conversations are important. These questions speak to purpose. What *are* we trying to achieve? I asked myself the same question regarding my involvement in the sport.

Since I was young, my father and I have gone to Melbourne one weekend every year, to watch as many matches as the fixture made possible. Games ceased to be played at suburban grounds like Whitten Oval, Victoria Park and Princess Park, and became confined to the MCG and the Docklands Stadium. The game transitioned from its historic mixture of chaos, skill, athleticism, and violence to a more structured, highly athletic, and patterned affair. Football became AFL. And a sport became an industry.

Dad used to take a hip flask to games and take a cheeky swig from time-to-time. It 'warmed the cockles of your heart', apparently. Around 15 years ago, we were at a game between Geelong and Collingwood, seated not far from the Collingwood cheer squad. Early in the first quarter, three security staff marched to the third row, spoke to a middle-aged lady sitting in the Collingwood cheer squad, and marched her out of the stadium. Apparently, she had taken a few sips from a hip flask.

Sport was now considered as just another industry, and the rights of those who sold alcohol at exorbitant prices in stadia had to be protected at all costs. This was justification enough to embarrass a supporter for whom the match was a weekly diversion and indulgence. A supporter who liked her footy with a little whiskey in the middle of winter. A supporter who was shamed in front of thousands for doing little wrong. A small thing, but a symptom of a society in which commercial considerations too often trump human ones.

Footy supporters had for a long time felt their sport was being taken away from them. By 2019, frustration was bubbling to the surface. Non-Victorian supporters were increasingly annoyed their former greats were scarcely recognised in AFL records. Fallen servicemen from states other than Victoria were not commemorated on ANZAC Day. Grand finals at the MCG offer a distinct advantage to Victorian sides.

Any doubts I had that this was the case were expelled the moment Collingwood ran onto the ground for the start of the 2018 grand final against West Coast. For all intents and purposes, it was Collingwood's home game, which rendered West Coast's victory that year even more meritorious. I was fortunate to attend three grand finals while working at Port Adelaide, but share the people's lament that the occasion is now largely a corporate affair that favours Establishment types who don't care much for either participating team.

The first grand final I attended was in 2016. Our guests had to leave the ground during the third quarter, and I escorted them to their cars outside the MCG. As I was returning to the stadium, the momentum was shifting away from pre-game favourites Sydney towards sentimental favourites Western Bulldogs. I spotted a middle-aged couple I guessed to be husband and wife, huddled together wearing Bulldogs colours, trying to catch a slither of the action through a glassed section of the stadium's high walls.

I hesitated, hovered, then offered them my pass into the ground. She asked if I had another ticket and was told I only had one. They looked at each other for a moment, before she declined the offer, saying, 'We want to experience this together.' AFL grand finals will return to their former beauty when there are more supporters like them inside the ground, and more people like me outside.

When the first games of the 2020 season were played in empty stadia, most lamented the absence of fans. It was eerie. A portent, perhaps, of what the sport is missing. It is time to put fans back in the centre of Australian football. AFL and its clubs will benefit from the loyalty of fans in 2020, but when it returns to business as usual, will the interests of fans be considered before those of broadcasters, sponsors, and players? Will the balance shift when it comes time to allocate grand final tickets?

Of course, you can't say these things when you work in 'the industry'. You can't say much, actually. I came to understand that as an employee of Port Adelaide I had to protect the interests and reputation of the club. Government funding for facilities is important. The Festival of Australia would not have been possible without a strong relationship with the Federal Government. But I don't feel that being an employee means that you automatically join the ranks of 'quiet Australians'.

I'm political. I care about what happens to our country. I also have a great respect for those sporting clubs that grasp that they serve a higher purpose and accept this responsibility. Historically, Liverpool Football Club has played such a role. In Australia, I have great respect for Richmond Football Club's principled stances on politically sensitive issues, such as Australia Day. By contrast, Port Adelaide appears to have become unsure of itself. If Richmond doesn't feel the need to decide between winning premierships and making its community proud, why should we?

In late 2019 and early 2020, Australia burned. It was a terrible summer. Human lives were lost. Homes were destroyed. Over one billion animals were eviscerated. On subjects serious or otherwise, it wasn't always clear what we were hurrying towards.

20 In the driver's seat

To accomplish great things, we must not only act, but also dream; not only plan, but also believe.

Anatole France

I watched the Showdown of 2020 in the Carlisle Hotel, Perth. A Western Australian supporters group assembled in a room to watch the game and were in full voice. I was no longer working for Port Adelaide and my family now called Perth home but the emotional implication in every kick, handball and mark remained exactly as it would have been had my situation not changed.

The Carlisle Hotel was an unfamiliar venue and it felt strange to watch a Showdown played in front of a handful of loud but physically distanced supporters. The jumper Port Adelaide took into battle represented the essence of my experience at Port Adelaide: a proud club determined to stay true to its traditions and identity while relentlessly pursuing progress.

The prominently displayed logo of 'MG' made the magnificent prison bars jumper appear even more beautiful in my eyes. The global automotive brand MG is owned by SAIC Motor, a Chinese state-owned automotive company. On a variety of levels, the jumper represented vindication for the club's fans, members, and administration.

Preparations for our anniversary year were made as Port Adelaide looked to define itself as a successful – traditional but modern – sporting organisation. It is, and must continue to be, a professional club of perpetual motion. If it stays in the past, it will degenerate and decay. It must honour the past, without compromising the future. Several issues needed to be resolved to satisfy both desires, which were also obligations and necessities.

The prison bars need a place in our present, and in our future. Port Adelaide understood that in accepting the invitation to join the AFL it accepted that some compromise would be necessary. In inviting Port Adelaide to join, the AFL surely also accepted that this club of unsurpassed sporting success would seek an appropriate expression of its heritage. The situation was more delicate as the league appeared beholden to the chairman of its most powerful club.

A compromise was agreed for the 2020 Showdown, but the situation will not go away. The ultimate outcome of the debate as to whether Port Adelaide has the right to wear its traditional jumper, fuelled by the predictable and petulant reaction of Collingwood President Eddie McGuire, will be another test of the extent to which we consider this competition national. Do we value each club and their heritage equally, or is it a competition of equals in the Orwellian sense, in which some are more equal than others?

Another threshold issue was addressed several months earlier when Tom Jonas was announced as the sole captain for the 2020 season. The tension between our desire to honour our heritage while embracing the needs of a modern sporting organisation has not been easy to resolve, but the club is moving towards an agreeable balance. Generous and smart off the field, uncompromising on it, was not Tom the embodiment of what the modern Port Adelaide aspired to be? It was incredibly exciting to see our captain wearing number one on his back and the prison bars on his chest as he ran onto the field on 28 March 2020.

If our strategy in China had been initially designed to bring new revenue without the attrition of traditional sporting assets, by 2020 it was clear that this objective did not reflect the club's reality. That is, we could not assume that all traditional assets would be sold to local companies. Indeed, the way in which the China strategy was judged internally ignored the half-million dollars in revenue that came directly from Cathay Pacific and Haneco, the latter owned and managed by the wonderful Nicho Teng.

The MG partnership was the result of almost 15 months of activity and effort. From late 2018 our commercial team had approached dealerships and contacts in the auto industry to introduce Port Adelaide to this emerging brand in the Australian market. Then, in 2019, SAIC's head office in China had made inquiries through three different avenues, each of which quickly became problematic. JUSS, the government-owned events company that ran the annual game in Shanghai, first made us aware of the interest of SAIC Motor, formerly Shanghai Automotive Industry Corporation. Despite our annual investment, however, we were not comfortable about their description of us. At one stage JUSS even suggested to SAIC they may be better served working with a 'bigger club'.

Another contact was made via an intermediary on our Chinese-language social media platform, WeChat. This initial contact very quickly went cold; their early appetite appearing to dissipate. Still another contact, with an Australian who had been active in China for many years, appeared positive but quickly turned sour. This guy, closely connected to a couple of other clubs and having done some work for the Crows, even derided us for having a 'FIFO' approach to China that would never work.

At no point did it appear likely that Port Adelaide would win this business. SAIC initially indicated their interest through various channels, and very soon had many suitors, including St Kilda, Essendon, and Collingwood – as well as the AFL itself. Outside the AFL, South Sydney Rabbitohs was well placed, and indeed our final opposition in an intensely competitive pitch.

When we first heard of their interest, we had no direct line of contact to SAIC. Strenuous efforts were taken to open a direct line of communication. We had its chairman invited to an exclusive luncheon with Graeme Meehan, Australia's outgoing Consul-General to Shanghai. They declined.

There was a lot at stake. Despite our profitable position in relation to our China engagement, and the ongoing relationship with CRED, losing a competitive pitch with a rival who had not invested as much in China would not have looked good. Dave Stevenson on behalf of the AFL advocated strongly on our behalf. The subliminal support of the Australian Government, combined with Dave's advocacy, may have confused matters for long enough to keep us in the fight.

On reflection, we handled the intermediaries poorly. In China, it is important to respect the role of an intermediary; they are being used for a reason. Advice from old China hands like Danny Armstrong was indispensable as we continued to learn how to navigate this fascinating but complex context. But two of the intermediaries who approached us had other agendas, and the third had a weaker connection to their head office. Once the centre of decision-making power moved from China to Australia, the natural advantage of being present and active in China was lost.

When the responsibility to make the decision moved to their Australian office, we tried a different tack. Robert Lu, a friend of recently appointed board member Andrew Day, had connections at SAIC. He identified Peter Ciao as the ultimate decision-maker and passed on his contact details.

In May 2018, KT met with Peter, the managing director of the Australian office, and Dave Stevenson. This trail then went cold and stayed cold for a long time. All looked lost when MG announced its sponsorship of the NBL and South East Melbourne Phoenix. But James Lindsay, our commercial GM, persisted, and his dogged persistence ultimately won this deal.

James had discovered that Port Adelaide remained in the running for major sponsorship in 2020, as did heavyweights Collingwood and Essendon. The Rabbitohs, we understood, were favourites. KT went to Sydney at late notice, asking Promise to return early from China where we were meeting with potential partners. He was keen to have her linguistic talent and cultural intelligence. KT presented. Time passed. The new year of 2020 began. We weren't feeling confident.

Over a beer in Hong Kong in late 2019, Denis Way suggested I meet Nick Raschella, a long-time PAFC member (a Club 1879 member to be precise), a man as committed to Port as one can be. I agreed, Denis pulled out his vintage Nokia, and called a number in Adelaide. 'It's midnight down there, Denis,' I protested. 'He'll be awake,' I was assured, and then I had the Nokia in my hand and Nick Raschella's voice in my ear. We met soon after and continued to talk.

In January 2020, he suggested we involve Darren Cahill and Simona Halep in a play designed to shift the dial. Darren was in Adelaide for the new Adelaide International tennis event, and happily obliged. We didn't want to associate Simona with MG, as she had a conflict with another car sponsor. Darren did a piece to camera, extolling the virtues of PAFC, which was sent directly to MG. The more subtle product placement was put on our social media channels.

The response was positive and rapid. Within 24 hours, there was an in-principal agreement. It was a great moment; the product of an absolute team effort, but also a tremendous individual performance by James Lindsay, who has delivered two joint major sponsors within a relatively short time. James's stewardship, along with KT's presentation, Promise's last-minute return from China, Darren's willingness to bend over backwards for his club, and Nick.

MG is the perfect fit for Port Adelaide. They will push us to be better. It is an ambitious company; Peter Ciao is an ambitious leader. I was present at the final negotiations that took place at Adelaide Oval, and the dinner that followed. We were asked, bluntly, when we will win our next premiership. For a club with a history of winning premierships, which is the core of who we are and central to our mission, his approach appeared to make some surprisingly uncomfortable. In view of performances in the early rounds of the 2020 season, the next premierships may come sooner than some had anticipated at the time.

MG expects success. If we are true to our history and mission, we should share and exceed this expectation. Anyone who feels uncomfortable about this expectation shouldn't be at Port Adelaide. It was exciting to hear someone affiliated with Port Adelaide demand success. We should hunger for such partnerships.

The partnership with MG was launched at Montefiore Hill, overlooking Adelaide Oval, on 25 February 2020. It was a beautiful day, and Peter Ciao delivered the perfect message: let's grow old together. The opportunity to realise a generational partnership with a global brand is here.

As always, we didn't have long to smell the coffee. The details of the contract had to be sorted, the execution phase had already begun. And novel coronavirus, as it was originally known, had started to impact our commercial and game-related plans for 2020. Only weeks from the first game, with six months of effort already in the bank from Shane and the team, cancellation loomed as a strong possibility. This job was never boring.

21 The virus

What's true of all the evils in the world is true of plague as well. It helps men to rise above themselves.

Albert Camus, *The Plague*

The year of Port Adelaide's 150th anniversary, 2020, is a year like no other. The origins of COVID-19 can be traced to 2019, but the extent of its impact was not apparent as our anniversary year started positively. We opened the season strongly against Gold Coast, following wins in our two pre-season games. A fantastic documentary about Port Adelaide's 150-year history, *Onwards to Victory,* appeared on the Seven Network immediately following the game.

From the time Port Adelaide held a spectacular gala dinner to celebrate the beginning of our anniversary year, however, it became increasingly clear that the effect of COVID-19 would not be temporary, nor trifling. The disruption it caused to Port Adelaide was at first creeping, then overwhelming.

First, our commercial activity in China was suspended. Then, the game scheduled to take place in Shanghai on 31 May was cancelled. Within 24 hours of the joint announcement that the Shanghai game had been cancelled, the Australian Government announced the Festival of Australia, too, would not proceed as planned in May. Minister Birmingham directly connected the cancellation of the AFL match and the

Government's decision to defer the FOA. All momentum for our project was immediately stalled.

Given the amount of planning and effort already expended on the game, and how well prepared we were, this was extremely disappointing for everyone involved. But these were relatively trivial considerations when considered alongside the challenges faced by many others. COVID-19 had cost people their lives, economies lay in ruin, and people's dreams deferred or forgotten.

Matters accelerated quickly. The sadness felt by those involved that Shanghai2020 was cancelled was soon overwhelmed by a realisation that the entire season would be compromised. The unappealing thought that games might be played to empty stadia was replaced by its reality, promptly followed by the announcement of an abridged season, and the suspension of the season until 11 June.

For the AFL and its clubs, such a long period of inactivity represented an existential dilemma. It is hard to imagine a league, which attracts the fourth largest per game in-stadium audience in world sport, could come under threat so quickly. The reality may be that a sport played uniquely in a modestly populated country will never warrant the broadcasting or sponsorship revenue that makes for a sustainable, secure model. If our sport fails to reach an international audience, it will ultimately court irrelevance. A matter of weeks separated hubris from the contemplation of financial ruin. Do these events, I wonder, strengthen the need for a globally relevant sport?

The future viability of the sport was probably not foremost in the minds of those employed in the industry who were made redundant, or stood down, as a result of the league's suspension. Several colleagues suffered this fate, as Port Adelaide reduced its active administrative team to 20-odd, from a staff of 70. All AFL clubs made similar reductions. This was the fate of most Australian businesses.

In normal circumstances, in the weeks following the victory against Gold Coast, our attention would have been fixed on a Showdown. Instead, Australia went into shutdown. And it was into this world, just four hours before the midday shutdown in South Australia, that my second son was born. Aurelien Thomas George Hunter, born 23 March 2020 – five years, to the day since I started working for Port Adelaide.

22 The future

The future belongs to those who believe in the beauty of their dreams.

Eleanor Roosevelt

In January 2020, I travelled to the United States to spend a week with the Washington Wizards. I packed books from American authors so I could enjoy the national literature as I was seeing the country. One book, which I evidently hadn't picked up for several years, held a special bookmark: the ticket to Port Adelaide v Collingwood at Adelaide Oval on 9 July 2015. I remember this game clearly; it was our first since the death of Phil Walsh. KT delivered a brilliant speech at the Chairman's event, during which a magpie circled overhead. I don't know how it got into the room, but it added poignance to an already poignant moment.

I make a habit of using train tickets, boarding passes, football or cinema tickets as bookmarks. And I keep them in the books after I finish reading them. When I pick up the book some years down the track, I connect my first experience of the book with a particular moment in time. When I reflect on the five years of this incredible adventure, I also recall the things that intellectually inspired me at the time.

A train ticket, which speaks of a journey from Shanghai to Hangzhou, for example, sits in *Flights* by Nobel Prize winner

Olga Tokarczuk. I recall the train trip, the jokes we made, the meetings we had before and after, and the thoughts the book had inspired at the time. Five years is a significant period in one's life. A lot of books were read, flights and train trips endured and enjoyed, meetings held, and games watched.

Some books remind me of the places I visited in China. Each time we travelled to Hangzhou, I read Nicholas Jose's *Bapo*. Every time I see the book on the shelf in my study, I recall sitting by the West Lake of Hangzhou early in the morning, pausing between passages of the book to enjoy the breathtaking beauty of the lake. Marco Polo may have got it right when he described Hangzhou as the most beautiful and splendid city in all the world.

The brief period spent in the United States in January 2020 prompted many reflections, about the way in which Port Adelaide is administered, and the opportunity it has to emerge as a modern, sophisticated organisation true to its mission of winning premierships and making the community proud. Are these merely words, the sum of which is better than not saying anything at all? Or are we willing to make the sacrifice required to sustain premiership success, and the courage to use the power of sport to improve lives in our community?

Everyone involved in Port Adelaide's push into China felt the intensity of the effort. Some were burnt by it. It has not been easy to develop partnerships in China, a country unfamiliar with and unenthusiastic about your core product. But there were unforgettable moments along the way, ties that bind and memories that endure.

In early December 2019, we put a sign outside my office that spoke to our three overarching objectives:

- $3 million
- Generational partners
- Global brand

We wanted to push towards a contribution of $3 million to Port Adelaide's bottom line. We wanted to develop long-term, mutually beneficial, generational partnerships. And we wanted to attract global brands, to help Port Adelaide Football Club become a global brand itself.

Reaction to MG becoming our Joint Major Sponsor was extremely positive. At last, many fans believed, there was a clear symbol of our success in China. They understood it would assist our club commercially. This reaction ignored the incredible contribution CRED had made to Port Adelaide. Though it did not feature on our jumper or coach's polo, CRED continued to contribute over a million dollars per year. The initial three-year agreement was extended by five years. By the end of this second term, CRED would have partnered with Port Adelaide for eight years, and Gui would be the largest investor in the club's history.

Even before the game in Shanghai was cancelled, I had decided to leave Port Adelaide. It was an extremely difficult decision, but the time was right. Five years is a long time to have such a singular, even obsessive, focus. When there came an opportunity for us to move to Perth, it was difficult to refuse, particularly considering the sacrifice Sally had made for me to pursue and sustain Port Adelaide's China dream. I won't ever forget her understanding when, in April 2016, I left for China only hours after she had missed qualifying for the national team, ending her dream of a third Olympics.

Nor will I forget what was achieved at Port Adelaide. The

memories remain vivid, the achievements real and hopefully lasting, the sense of gratitude great. The five years have been unforgettable. The fondest memories are of the earliest days, when a few people inspired by a vision and dedicated to achieving something extraordinary, somehow came together. I recall the first trip to Hong Kong. The first beer with Denis. The first lunch with Zhang Bin. The Aboriginal boys dancing on the Great Wall.

Vivid remains the memory of the first meeting with Gui. Firm was my belief that a deal was there to be done that would change Port Adelaide forever. In many ways, the period separating then from now has been a constant chase for a moment that would bring a similar feeling of excitement, of ebullience, born of deep desire to contribute something special to the enviable tradition of Port Adelaide Football Club, an institution I feel incredibly privileged to have served.

Acknowledgements

This project would not have been possible without the patience and commitment of Wakefield Press. I would particularly like to thank Julia Beaven.

Thanks also to my former colleagues who took time to read the manuscript so I could check my experience against theirs. There are too many to name, but I especially thank Xu Nuo for her time and thoughts.

Past and present Australian Government officials also contributed their perspectives. This was very much a Port Adelaide story, but it was important to understand what was occurring on the other side. This would not have been possible without their contributions.

Finally, I would like to acknowledge my wife, Sally, for her support. Without her, this story would not have been lived, let alone told!